AF819601

Following **NEP 2020**

NCERT PRACTICE

Work BOOK

English Class 7

Following NEP 2020

NCERT PRACTICE Work BOOK

English Class 7

Honeycomb Textbook (Prose & Poetry)
An Alien Hand (Supplementary Reader)

As Per Latest NCERT (with Rationalised Content)

Emmanuel D'Souza
Gloria D'Souza

arihant
Arihant Prakashan (School Division Series)

arihant

Arihant Prakashan (School Division Series)

Administrative & Production Offices

Regd. Office

'Ramchhaya' 4577/15, Agarwal Road, Darya Ganj, New Delhi -110002
Tele: 011- 47630600, 43518550

Head Office

Kalindi, TP Nagar, Meerut (UP) - 250002
Tel: 0121-7156203, 7156204

Sales & Support Offices

Agra, Ahmedabad, Bengaluru, Bareilly, Chennai, Delhi, Guwahati, Hyderabad, Jaipur, Jhansi, Kolkata, Lucknow, Nagpur & Pune.

PO No : TXT-XX-XXXXXXX-X-XX

Published by Arihant Publications (India) Ltd.

For further information about the books published by Arihant, log on to www.arihantbooks.com or e-mail at info@arihantbooks.com

Follow us on

9 789327 196986

PRODUCTION TEAM

Publishing Managers
Keshav Mohan, Amit Verma

Project Coordinator
Manju

Cover Designer
Bilal Hashmi

Inner Designer
Ankit Saini

Proof Readers
Akash Agarwal, Bhawna Madrey

Workbook, Why?

"Knowledge will not be with you for Long Unless You Practice "

This quotation answer the above question 'Workbook, Why ?' perfectly, the explanation is given in the text given below.

NCERT textbooks are the only textbooks, which have been prepared according to National Curriculum Framework, which discourages the idea of rote learning and recommends that students' life at school must be linked to their life outside the school. NCERT textbooks focus on inculcating creativity & initiative in the students to make them participants in learning not just a receiver of a one-way communication.

ONLY COMPLETE WORKBOOK BASED ON NCERT

Keeping the importance of NCERT textbooks in mind we have prepared this Workbook, strictly based on NCERT content, this Workbook will complement NCERT by providing practice to help reinforce the material given in each chapter of NCERT textbook. This is the only Workbook, which covers English syllabus completely, it has all the four sections; Literature, Grammar, Writing & Reading.

WORKBOOK– PURPOSE, USE & FEATURES

This Workbook, through its **numerous exercises** having different **variety of questions** covering **practical importance** of English & **Day-to-Day communication**, will prove to be **equally useful** for both, **Classroom** and at **Home**. One more purpose of this Workbook is to provide the students a **systematic practice** of the content taught in the class and what they study in the textbooks.

Some special features of this workbook are

- Complete coverage of all the sections; **Literature**, **Grammar**, **Writing** & **Reading**.
- Complete coverage of all the chapters in a comprehensive manner.
- Different variety of questions; Fill in the Blanks, True-False, Matching, Multiple Choice Questions, Differentiate between, Define the following, One word for, Odd One Out, Very Short Answer, Short Answer, Long Answer Type HOTs, VBQs etc.

WORKBOOK– DESIGNED TO IMPROVE SUBJECT ABILITIES

All the material given in this workbook is tailored to suit subject content with equal support on learning, which will surely help students to boost their abilities and confidence in the subject.

We look forward for the feedback from students, teachers and parents for the further improvement of the contents of this book. We will try to update the contents according to your feedback in further editions of this Workbook.

The Publisher

Contents

TABLE FOR RATIONALISED CONTENT

753 - Honeycomb

Chapter	Old NCERT Page No.	Dropped Topics/Chapters
Unit 8 : Fire : Friend and Foe	114-122	Full Chapter
Unit 9 : A Bicycle in Good Repair	126-136	Full Chapter
Unit 10 : The Story of Cricket	139-151	Full Chapter

754 - An Alien Hand (Supplementary Reader)

Chapter	Old NCERT Page No.	Dropped Topics/Chapters
Chapter 3 : The Desert	15-19	Full Chapter
Chapter 4 : The Cop and the Anthem	20-29	Full Chapter
Chapter 6 : I Want Something in a Cage	36-42	Full Chapter

[Chapter 1]

Three Questions

Leo Tolstoy

Very Short Answer Type Questions

1 How many questions did the king have?

2 What reward did the king promise to anyone who answered his questions?

3 What was the hermit known for?

4 What did the king do with the spade?

5 Who wounded the bearded man?

6 Why did the bearded man faint and fall on the ground?

Short Answer Type Questions

1 How did the king pursue the hermit to answer his questions?

2 Describe the appearance of the hermit.

3 Did the king save the injured man's life? Explain.

4 Why did the bearded man want to kill the king?

Long Answer Type Questions

1 What were the various answers given by the wise men to the king's first question?

2 What was the intention of the bearded man? What happened to him? How did the king make peace with him?

3 Did the hermit answer all the three questions? What were his answers?

4 The king was kind enough to forgive the bearded man. What did this act suggest about his character? **(VBQ)**

Extract Based Questions

Directions *Read the extracts carefully and answer the following questions.*

1 As the answers to his questions were so different, the king was not satisfied and gave no reward. Instead, he decided to seek the advice of a certain hermit, who was widely known for his wisdom. The hermit lived in a wood which he never left. He saw no one but simple people and so the king put on ordinary clothes. Before he reached the hermit's hut the king left his horse with his bodyguard and went on alone.

(i) What did the king do before entering the hermit's hut?

(ii) Why did the king decide to seek the hermit's advice?

(iii) How did the king dress up himself before meeting the hermit?

(iv) Who was not satisfied with the answers?

(a) Hermit ☐ (b) Bodyguard ☐

(c) King ☐ (d) Horse ☐

(v) Choose synonym for the word 'advice'.

(a) Suggestion ☐ (b) Reward ☐

(c) Clothes ☐ (d) Alone ☐

2 The man felt better and asked for something to drink. The king brought fresh water and gave it to him. By this time the sun had set and the air was cool. The king with the hermit's help carried the wounded man into the hut and laid him on the bed. The man closed his eyes and lay quiet. The king, tired by his walk and the work he had done, lay down on the floor and slept through the night. When he awoke, it was several minutes before he could remember where he was or who the strange bearded man lying on the bed was.

(i) Do you think the king was tired? If yes, why?

(ii) Why did they bring the wounded man into the hut?

(iii) What happened immediately after the king woke up?

(iv) A word that means 'unusual' or 'surprising' is

(a) tired ☐ (b) slept ☐

(c) strange ☐ (d) hermit ☐

(v) Who brought fresh water for the wounded man?

(a) King ☐ (b) Hermit ☐

(c) Soldiers ☐ (d) Doctors ☐

True or False

1 The hermit was old and weak. ☐

2 The king decided to seek the advice of a magician. ☐

3 The bearded man wanted to kill the king. ☐

4 The king killed the bearded man out of anger. ☐

Imagination Based Questions

1 In the story, the king forgives the bearded man who came with an intention of seeking revenge. Imagine yourself in place of the king, would you have forgiven the bearded man or punished him?

2 Imagine yourself as the hermit in the story. Share your experience of meeting the king and helping him with his questions.

[Chapter 2]

A Gift of Chappals

Vasantha Surya

Very Short Answer Type Questions

1 Why did Mridu visit Rukku Manni's house?

2 What happened when Mridu entered the house?

3 Where did the children (Ravi and Meena) find the kitten?

4 Where did the small kitten lay comfortably?

5 What was the full name of the kitten? What was its other name?

6 Who is Lalli? What was she doing in the story – A Gift of Chappals?

7 Why didn't Ravi repeat every message of his mother to the beggar?

8 Why all the children were ready to give their slippers to the beggar?

9 Ravi could not give his own slippers to the beggar. Why?

10 What was the cost of the chappals, according to the music teacher?

Short Answer Type Questions

1 Why did the large black slippers kept in the verandah appear grey?

2 Why was it difficult for Ravi to arrange milk for the kitten?

3 What did Ravi mention about Mahabalipuram?

4 What made Mridu startled and Mahendravarma frighten?

5 What comparison did Ravi make between Lalli and the music-master when they were playing the violin?

6 How did the beggar make himself comfortable in the garden?

7 Why did the beggar quickly vanish from the scene after wearing a pair of slippers?

8 Why did the music-master's eyes lit up on seeing Gopu Mama's chappals?

9 Who gave the reference of 'Karna' in the chapter and why?

10 Who was being compared to a holy monkey in the chapter 'A Gift of Chappals' and why?

Long Answer Type Questions

1 How did the little kitty (kitten) get its name?

2 Describe the appearance of the music teacher in the chapter 'A Gift of Chappals'.

3 The children gave away a pair of slippers, belonging to the music teacher, to the beggar with sores on his feet. What does this incidence tell us about the nature of the children? Explain. **(VBQ)**

Extract Based Questions

Directions *Read the extracts carefully and answer the following questions.*

1 The beggar opened his eyes very wide and gazed at each of the children one by one. "The ladies of this house," he said, at last, in a voice choked with feeling, "are very kind souls. I have kept my body and soul together on their generosity for a whole week. I cannot believe that they would turn me away." He raised his voice. "Amma! Amma – oh!" Sad his wail might be, but it certainly wasn't feeble. It began in a deep, strong rumble somewhere in his withered belly and came booming out of his mouth, with its few remaining teeth stained brown with betel-chewing.

(i) Why did the beggar say that the ladies were kind souls?

(ii) Who apparently became sad in the above lines?

(iii) Why did the beggar gaze at the children?

(iv) Choose synonym of the word 'generosity'.

(a) Casual ☐ (b) Scarcity ☐
(c) Kind ☐ (d) Rude ☐

(v) Choose noun of the word 'sad'.

(a) Sadness ☐ (b) Happy ☐
(c) Sadly ☐ (d) Kind ☐

2 When he had clattered off in his new chappals, she said, "Mridu, come in and have some tiffin. Honestly, how do you children think of such things? Thank God your Gopu Mama doesn't wear his chappals to work..." As she walked towards the kitchen with Mridu and Meena, she suddenly began to laugh. "But he's always in such a hurry to throw off his shoes and socks and get into his chappals as soon as he comes home. What's your mama going to say this evening when I tell him I gave his chappals to music-master?"

(i) Why did Rukku Manni start laughing?

(ii) Who is Gopu Mama?

(iii) What did Rukku Manni mean when she said how could the children think of such things?

(iv) The word 'suddenly' is a

(a) Noun ☐ (b) Verb ☐
(c) Adjective ☐ (d) Adverb ☐

(v) Choose antonym of the word 'honest'.

(a) Naughty ☐ (b) Rush ☐

(c) Dishonest ☐ (d) Curious ☐

True or False

1 Ravi dragged Mridu to the backyard of the house. ☐

2 Paati sent a glass full of milk for the kitten. ☐

3 Ravi was learning to play the violin. ☐

4 Lalli was wearing a gold chain and a diamond ring. ☐

5 Rukku Manni was happy after Ravi gave a pair of slippers to the beggar. ☐

Imagination Based Questions

1 Do you think its possible to hide a secret from your parents? Share one of your experience and whether you succeeded or not?

____

____

____

2 Imagine what would have happened in the story when Gopu Mama returns home.

____

____

____

3 Suppose a beggar comes to your door and asks for a pair of slippers. Whose slippers would you give away and why? Do you think you would receive a scolding from your mother?

____

____

____

Chapter 3

Gopal and the Hilsa-Fish

Very Short Answer Type Questions

1 What was it the season for?

2 Who were discussing the Hilsa-fish inside the palace?

3 What did the courtier comment about Gopal inside the palace?

4 What did the king ask Gopal after he entered the palace?

Short Answer Type Questions

1 How did Gopal prepare himself to buy the Hilsa-fish?

2 Do you think Gopal's wife was shocked to find him dressed up in a weird way? Give reasons to support your answer.

3 What was the reaction of the public after Gopal changed his appearance?

4 How did Gopal manage to enter inside the palace?

Long Answer Type Questions

1. Why did the king lose his temper?

2. Why no one asked anything from Gopal about the Hilsa-fish?

3. Do you think Gopal was intelligent and clever? What do you learn from the chapter - 'Gopal and the Hilsa-fish'? **(VBQ)**

Extract Based Questions

Directions *Read the extracts carefully and answer the following questions.*

1 "I'm sorry I lost my temper it is the season for Hilsa-fish and no one... not even Gopal can stop anyone from talking about Hilsa-fish. Not even for five minutes!"

(i) Who is the speaker of the above lines and who is he speaking to?

(ii) What issue is the speaker referring to?

(iii) How did the listener react to the problem?

(iv) Who is Gopal?

(a) Fisherman ☐ (b) Majesty ☐

(c) Courtier ☐ (d) Soldier ☐

(v) A word that refers to an 'upset mind' is

(a) tired ☐ (b) calm ☐

(c) guilty ☐ (d) temper ☐

2 "Strangely enough no one seems to be interested in Hilsa-fish today! From the market to the palace and in the court, not a soul has spoken a word about Hilsa-fish."

(i) Who is the speaker and where did he go?

(ii) Why is no one interested in the Hilsa-fish?

(iii) What happened when Gopal reached the court?

(iv) Choose synonym of the word 'curious'.

(a) Uninvolved ☐ (b) Interested ☐

(c) Incurious ☐ (d) Strangely ☐

(v) The words 'soul' and 'sole' have similar sound, they are called

(a) Homophones ☐ (b) Homonyms ☐

(c) Antonyms ☐ (d) Synonyms ☐

True or False

1 Gopal's wife smeared herself with ash. ☐

2 Gopal could not buy a huge Hilsa-fish. ☐

3 The king lost his temper initially. ☐

4 The king congratulated Gopal. ☐

5 Gopal dressed up in a ridiculous manner. ☐

Imagination Based Questions

1 Imagine yourself in place of Gopal. What idea would you have used if the king gave you a similar challenge?

2 Suppose you were one of the courtiers in the king's palace. What would've been your reaction and the reaction of other courtiers when Gopal was brought before the king?

Chapter 4

The Ashes that Made Trees Bloom

William Elliot Griffis

Very Short Answer Type Questions

1 What was the occupation of the old man?

2 Why did the good couple love their dog unconditionally?

3 What was the name of the dog in the chapter— 'The Ashes that Made Trees Bloom'?

4 Why did the white heron walk along with the good old man?

5 What made the wicked old man and his wife persuade the dog?

6 Who found a dead kitten in the ground?

7 Who peeped through the window when the good old couple was making rice pastry and bean sauce?

8 Did the wicked couple succeed in making rice pastry and bean sauce?

9 Why did the good old man ask for the ashes?

10 What happened when the good old man sprinkled a pinch of ashes on the cherry tree?

11 The delighted daimio ordered the train to be stopped. What was the cause?

12 What was the custom which people needed to follow at the time of daimios?

Short Answer Type Questions

1 How did the good couple feed their dog?

2 What was the attitude of the wicked couple towards dogs?

3 How did the old man become rich for the first time?

4 After becoming rich for the first time how did the old couple share their riches with others?

5 Who killed the dog? What was the reason behind taking such an extreme step?

6 What did the spirit of the dog tell the good old man for the first time?

7 After collecting the ashes of the mill, why did the old man take his wife to the garden?

8 What happened when the wicked old man threw a handful of ashes over the cherry tree?

9 Why did the daimio reward the good old man?

10 At the end of the story how did the fate of the good old couple differ from that of the wicked old couple?

Long Answer Type Questions

1 The good old man was deeply moved by the death of his dog. How did he mourn this loss?

2 The dog appeared to the good old man twice in his dreams. What did the dog suggest both the times? Explain.

3 What did the good old man do when the daimio's procession passed along the high road?

4 Do you think the dog remained faithful to his master in context of the chapter 'The Ashes that Made Trees Bloom'? Give reasons to support your answer. **(VBQ)**

Extract Based Questions

Directions *Read the extracts carefully and answer the following questions.*

1 One day the dog came running to him, putting his paws against his legs and motioning with his head to some spot behind. The old man at first thought his pet was only playing and did not mind it. But the dog kept on whining and running to and fro for some minutes. Then the old man followed the dog a few yards to a place where the animal began a lively scratching. Thinking it was possibly a buried bone or bit of fish the old man struck his hoe in the Earth, when, lo! A pile of gold gleamed before him.

(i) What did the good old man think about his dog for the first time?

(ii) Why did the dog keep on whining and running to and fro?

(iii) How did the good old man discover a pile of gold?

(iv) Synonym of the word 'whine' is

(a) laugh ☐ (b) whimper ☐

(c) smile ☐ (d) play ☐

(v) Choose the meaning of the word 'scratch'.

(a) Cut with a sharp weapon ☐

(b) Chop off ☐

(c) Mark the surface with a sharp or pointed object ☐

(d) To run along with someone ☐

2 "Quick, wife, hand me the spade and hoe!" cried the greedy old fool, as he danced with joy. Then the covetous old fellow, with a spade, and the old crone, with a hoe, began to dig; but there was nothing but a dead kitten, the smell of which made them drop their tools and shut their noses.

Furious at the dog, the old man kicked and beat him to death, and the old woman finished the work by nearly chopping off his head with the sharp hoe. They then flung him into the hole and heaped the Earth over his carcass.

(i) Who is asking for a spade and hoe in the above lines?

(ii) What made the old greedy couple drop their tools?

(iii) What happened to the dog?

(iv) The word 'nearly' is a

(a) Noun ☐ (b) Verb ☐

(c) Adjective ☐ (d) Adverb ☐

(v) Choose antonym of the word 'dead'.

(a) Alive ☐ (b) Sharp ☐

(c) Chop off ☐ (d) Alone ☐

True or False

1 The wicked old man and his wife were very sensitive and kind towards the dog. ☐

2 The owner of the dog heard about the death of his pet and mourned its death. ☐

3 The envious neighbour did not peep in at the window when the boiled beans were being ground. ☐

4 The daimio thanked the good old man and presented him with silk robes, sponge-cake, fans and other rewards. ☐

5 The good old man angrily asked for the ashes. ☐

Fill in the Blanks

1 The dog ________ the old man daily to the fields.

2 The greedy old woman ________ the dog's head with a sharp hoe.

3 After ____________ home, the old man took his wife to the garden.

4 The old man happily ____________ home to share his joy with his dear old wife.

Imagination Based Questions

1 People often treat pet animals as family members, loving them unconditionally. How would you feel and treat it if you had an elephant as your pet?

____

____

____

2 Imagine yourself as a neighbour of the good old couple. You come to know how the couple made a fortune because of their pet dog. What would you have done in such a situation?

____

____

____

3 Suppose one day you get lucky like the good old man and accumulate a lot of gold and riches. What would you do with the wealth?

____

____

____

[Chapter 5]

Quality

John Galsworthy

Very Short Answer Type Questions

1. Where was Mr. Gessler's shop located?

2. What did the author mention about boots made by Mr. Gessler?

3. Why didn't the author visit the shop for about two years?

4. Why did it appear to the author that Mr. Gessler's elder brother was handling the shop?

5. For how long did the author go to abroad?

6. Mr. Gessler's name was missing from the shop. What was the reason?

Short Answer Type Questions

1. How was Mr. Gessler's shop different from other shops?

2. What did Mr. Gessler discuss about his trade with the author?

3. Why did the author order several pairs of shoes? Did he want to help Mr. Gessler? Why?

4. What did the young man tell the author about Mr. Gessler?

5. What would Mr. Gessler do day and night according to the young man?

Long Answer Type Questions

1 How did Mr. Gessler die? Was he a hardworking man? Give reasons to support your answer.

2 Do you think that Mr. Gessler was a master bootmaker but lacked competitive business skills of big firms? Comment on the statement with reference to the story.

3 Do you think quality should be the priority while purchasing any article? Explain in context of the chapter 'Quality'. **(VBQ)**

Extract Based Questions

Directions *Read the extracts carefully and answer the following questions.*

1 Without a word he would leave me retiring whence he came, or into the other portion of the shop, and I would continue to rest in the wooden chair inhaling the incense of his trade. Soon he would come back, holding in his hand a piece of gold-brown leather. With eyes fixed on it he would remark, "What a beautiful biece!" When I too had admired it, he would speak again. "When do you wand dem?" And I would answer, "Oh! As soon as you conveniently can." And he would say, "Tomorrow fordnighd?" Or if he were his elder brother: "I will ask my brudder."

(i) Who is 'he' in the above lines? What was his profession?

(ii) Who is 'I' in the above lines? What was his purpose behind coming to the shop?

(iii) When does the author want his boots?

(iv) The synonym of 'admire' is

(a) praise (b) stay

(c) force (d) pick

(v) The antonym of the word 'continue' is

(a) convenient (b) piece

(c) remark (d) discontinue

2. Once (once only) I went absent-mindedly into his shop in a pair of boots bought in an emergency at some large firm. He took my order without showing me any leather and I could feel his eyes penetrating the inferior covering of my foot. At last he said, "Dose are nod my boods." The tone was not of anger, nor of sorrow, not even of contempt, but there was in it something quiet that froze the blood. He put his hand down and pressed a finger on the place where the left boot was not quite comfortable.

(i) Why did Mr. Gessler press his finger on the boot?

(ii) Do you think Mr. Gessler was happy with the author's boots?

(iii) Who bought a pair of boots from a large firm?

(iv) The word 'absent-mindedly' is a

(a) Noun ☐ (b) Verb ☐
(c) Adjective ☐ (d) Adverb ☐

(v) A word that means 'a serious, unexpected and often dangerous situation' is

(a) contempt ☐ (b) emergency ☐
(c) comfort ☐ (d) quite ☐

True or False

1 Mr. Gessler lived with his elder brother in the shop. ☐
2 The author did not like the boots made by Mr Gessler. ☐
3 Mr. Gessler died due to brain cancer. ☐
4 There was a young man with an English face in shop. ☐
5 Mr. Gessler advertised for his boots to boost sales. ☐

Imagination Based Questions

1 Do you think making/designing an item such as shoes involves artistic skills? Imagine yourself as a shoemaker. What important points will you keep in mind while making a pair of shoes?

2 Suppose you plan to start a business with your brother or sister, like Mr. Gessler and his elder brother from the story. What would it be and why?

Chapter 6

Expert Detectives

Sharada Dwivedi

Very Short Answer Type Questions

1 Nishad was also called 'Seven'. Why?

2 Why Maya did not consider Mr. Nath to be poor?

3 How does Mr. Nath pay to get food from outside according to Maya?

4 What did Maya mention about Mr. Nath's scars?

5 Why did Seven give a bar of chocolate to Mr. Nath?

6 What made Maya pat on Nishad's back?

7 What doubt did the children have regarding Mr. Nath's real name?

8 Maya thinks Mr. Nath is mannerless. What is the reason behind it?

9 Where does Mr. Nath live? Does anyone visit him?

10 What could be the possible reason behind Mr. Nath bribing Ramesh?

11 What was fact number 7 as per the list made by Maya in the chapter 'Expert Detectives'?

Short Answer Type Questions

1 What did Maya and Seven's mother tell about Mr. Nath? How did Mr. Nath and their mother know each other?

2 What did Ramesh tell Seven about Mr. Nath's food habits?

3 What did Maya mention about the Hyderabadi housebreaker?

4 How did Nishad and Maya get an unexpected holiday?

5 Why did Maya prepare a list of all the facts about Mr. Nath?

6 Why did Nishad become angry? What did he tell Maya?

7 Why didn't Nishad pay attention to Maya's list of facts?

8 How did both the children begin to argue over Mr. Nath?

9 Maya did not want Nishad to befriend Mr. Nath. What was the reason?

10 Do you think the story 'Expert Detectives' had an abrupt ending? Give reasons to support your answer.

Long Answer Type Questions

1 How was Seven's chance encounter with Mr. Nath on the day he had gone to his Mamma's clinic at Girgaum?

2 Who visited Mr. Nath on Sundays? What do we know about him?

3 Do you think it is right to judge a person without knowing him/her properly? Give reasons to support your answer. **(VBQ)**

Extract Based Questions

Directions *Read the extracts carefully and answer the following questions.*

1 On the Monday following Mamma's birthday, Seven went alone with her to the clinic at Girgaum as I was spending the evening with a school friend. When they returned, Nishad told me he'd been to see Mr. Nath and I felt most annoyed that I hadn't been there. Seven has been quite upset about Mr. Nath's gaunt appearance and was sure that he was starving. He told me that he had knocked loudly on Mr. Nath's door that evening and said, "Open the door quickly, Mr. Nath."

(i) Why did Maya feel annoyed?

(ii) What made Nishad upset?

(iii) What was Maya doing when Nishad visited the clinic?

(iv) Choose the antonym of the word 'starving'.

(a) Hungry ☐ (b) Empty ☐ (c) Well-fed ☐ (d) Craving ☐

(v) Choose synonym of the word 'gaunt'.

(a) Thin ☐ (b) Strong ☐ (c) Strength ☐ (d) Skeleton ☐

2 "Ramesh told me something very strange, Maya," Seven added. "Almost every Sunday, he carries two lunches to Mr. Nath's room and the same man is with him each time. He's tall, fair, stout and wears spectacles. Ramesh says his visitor talks a lot, unlike Mr. Nath who hardly speaks."
"Well done, Nishad," I told him. "Now that we've made some progress with our inquires, we'll have to sort out all the facts like expert detectives so that we can trap the crook."

(i) Why did Ramesh carry two lunches to Mr. Nath's room on Sundays?

(ii) Who comes to Mr. Nath's room on every Sunday? Briefly describe his appearance.

(iii) How did Maya react when Nishad informs her about the man?

(iv) The word 'progress' is a

(a) Adjective ☐ (b) Noun ☐ (c) Adverb ☐ (d) Pronoun ☐

(v) A word that means 'dishonest or criminal' is

(a) crook ☐ (b) stout ☐ (c) strange ☐ (d) sort ☐

True or False

1 Nishad paid full attention to Maya's list of facts. ☐

2 Maya wanted Nishad to be friendly with Mr. Nath. ☐

3 According to Maya, Mr. Nath got millions of rupees stashed away somewhere in his room. ☐

4 Mr. Nath was under Seven's mother's medical treatment. ☐

5 Kids and some of the grown-ups were very friendly with Mr. Nath. ☐

Fill in the Blanks

1 I am ________ whether Mr. Nath is a criminal.

2 My mother ________ called the police to the crime scene.

3 Nishad ________ walked out of the house.

4 I do not know the outcome of our ________ .

5 The police has started their ________ .

Imagination Based Questions

1 Imagine yourself in place of Maya or Seven. What if you have a mysterious neighbour like Mr. Nath, how will you investigate about him?

2 In the story Mr. Nath, lives alone and does not have any friend. The children think of various reasons behind his mysterious lifestyle. Who do you think Mr. Nath is?

3 Do you like reading detective stories/novels? Think of a story imagining yourself as a detective trying to solve a murder mystery.

Chapter 7

The Invention of Vita-Wonk

Roald Dahl

Very Short Answer Type Questions

1 What was Mr. Wonka's new recipe?

2 How did Mr. Wonka manage to rush all over the world?

3 What did Mr. Wonka mention about Bristlecone pine?

4 Why did Mr. Wonka search for very old and ancient animals?

5 What did Mr. Wonka collect from Arabia?

Short Answer Type Questions

1 Which two questions did Mr. Wonka ask himself before beginning to invent Vita-Wonk?

2 What was the usage of the Great Glass Elevator? How did it help Mr. Wonka?

3 What was unique about Venomous Squerkle?

4 Why did the author call Oompa-Loompa volunteer a brave person?

5 Describe how a 20 year-old person was transformed into a 75 year-old fellow.

Long Answer Type Questions

1 What was the problem with Wonka-Vite? How did it lead to the invention of Vita-Wonk?

2 How did Mr. Wonka invent Vita-Wonk? Mention all the steps involved in producing this liquid.

3 Do you think it is possible to prepare liquid which can make a youth an old man? Give reasons to support your answer. **(VBQ)**

Extract Based Questions

Directions *Read the extracts carefully and answer the following questions.*

1 "Right you are, Charlie! But what kind of a tree? Not the Douglas fir. Not the oak. Not the cedar. No, no, my boy. It is a tree called the Bristlecone pine that grows upon the slopes of Wheeler Peak in Nevada, USA. You can find Bristlecone Pines on Wheeler Peak today that are over 4000 years old! This is fact, Charlie. Ask any dendrochronologist you like (and look that word up in the dictionary when you get home, will you please?). So that started me off. I jumped into the Great Glass Elevator and rushed all over the world collecting special items from the oldest living things...

(i) Who is 'you' in the above lines?

(ii) Where does the Bristlecone pine grow?

(iii) Name all the trees mentioned in the above paragraph.

(iv) Choose the comparative degree for the word 'old'.

(a) Oldest ☐ (b) Oldly ☐

(c) Older ☐ (d) Oddly ☐

(v) Choose adjective of the word 'home'.

(a) House ☐ (b) Building ☐

(c) Homesickness ☐ (d) Homely ☐

2 "All over the world, Charlie," Mr. Wonka went on "I tracked down very old and ancient animals and took an important little bit of something from each one of them a hair or an eyebrow or sometimes it was no more than an ounce or two of the jam scrapped from between its toes while it was sleeping.

I tracked down the Whistle-pig, the Bobolink, the Skrock, the Pollyfrog, the Giant curlicue, the Stinging slug and the venomous squerkle who can spit poison right into your eye from fifty yards away. But there's no time to tell you about them all now, Charlie. Let me just say quickly that in the end, after lots of boiling and bubbling and mixing and testing in my Inventing Room, I produced one tiny cupful of oily black liquid and gave four drops of it to a brave twenty-year-old Oompa-Loompa volunteer to see what happened?"

(i) Why Mr. Wonka has no time to explain the entire method?

____

(ii) What did Mr. Wonka produce at the end?

____

(iii) How many drops of the liquid were given to the volunteer?

____

(iv) Tick one word for 'a substance capable of causing illness or death of a living organism'.

(a) Quick ☐ (b) Invent ☐

(c) Liquid ☐ (d) Poison ☐

(v) Choose noun for the word 'produce'.

(a) Produced ☐ (b) Production ☐

(c) Proper ☐ (d) Propellant ☐

True or False

1 The 25-year-old Oompa-Loompa volunteer invented the Vita-Wonk. ☐

2 Mr. Wonka already made a discovery and was ready for another one. ☐

3 Mr. Wonka collected an egg laid by a 20-year-old tortoise. ☐

4 Mr. Wonka gave ten drops of black liquid to the brave volunteer. ☐

5 Mr. Wonka collected the tail of a 207-year-old giant rat from Tibet. ☐

Imagination Based Questions

1 Imagine yourself as the person who becomes minus 87 due to the consumption of Wonka-Vite, which makes people younger. How would you feel after you are finally born and what would you do?

2 You get a chance to visit Mr. Wonka's inventing room and look at the interesting ingredients for various experiments and inventions. What secret recipe would you like to invent and why?

3 Imagine yourself as Charlie. How would you feel meeting a great scientist such as Mr. Wonka?

4 If you get a chance to travel in Mr. Wonka's Great Glass Elevator which are the places you would like to visit and why?

Poetry

(Poem 1)

The Squirrel

Mildred Bowers Armstrong

Very Short Answer Type Questions

1 Where does the squirrel live?

2 What does the squirrel generally like to do?

3 What did the squirrel eat on the tree?

Short Answer Type Questions

1 What is the appearance of the squirrel?

2 Who was observing the squirrel and what did he observe?

Long Answer Type Question

1 A squirrel is swift and energetic going up and down the trees, playing the whole day. According to you, what is the importance of playing and other forms of physical activity in a child's life? **(VBQ)**

Extract Based Questions

Directions *Read the extracts given below carefully and answer the following questions.*

1

He wore a question mark for tail,
An overcoat of gray
He sat up straight to eat a nut.

(i) Name the poem and the poet of the above lines.

(ii) Briefly describe the tail of the squirrel.

(iii) What does the 'overcoat' refer to?

(iv) Choose antonym of the word 'straight'.

(a) Curvy ☐ (b) Direct ☐
(c) Uniform ☐ (d) Linear ☐

(v) The word 'overcoat' is a

(a) Verb ☐ (b) Adjective ☐
(c) Adverb ☐ (d) Noun ☐

2

He liked to tease and play,
And if we ran around his tree,
He went the other way.

(i) Who liked to tease?

(ii) What is the tree to the squirrel?

(iii) "And if we ran around his tree". Who is 'we' here?

(iv) Choose the synonym of the word 'around' .

(a) Across ☐ (b) Between ☐
(c) Near ☐ (d) Under ☐

(v) Who went on the other way?

(a) Poet ☐ (b) Squirrel ☐
(c) Tree ☐ (d) Children ☐

Imagination Based Questions

1 Imagine yourself as a squirrel. How does it feel to go up and down the trees whole day and being free to roam everywhere?

2 Suppose one day you wake up and find a tail growing out of your body. What will you do?

3 Go to a garden and observe the activities of a squirrel. Do you think that there are more activities which can be added to the poem?

[Poem 2]

The Rebel

DJ Enright

Very Short Answer Type Questions

1 What is the reaction of the rebel when everybody talks during the class?

2 What provokes the rebel to wear fantastic clothes?

3 What does the rebel do in the company of dog lovers?

4 When does the rebel need the rainfall?

5 When does the rebel prefer to say 'yes'?

Short Answer Type Questions

1 State when would the rebel grow his hair long and short.

2 Give three instances when the rebel does the opposite of what others do.

3 State when would the rebel give negative and positive replies.

Long Answer Type Questions

1 What do you think is the message that the poet is trying to convey through the poem?

2 Do you think the rebel is a curse for the society? Give reasons to support your answer. **(VBQ)**

Extract Based Questions

Directions *Read the extracts given below carefully and answer the following questions.*

1

When everybody wears a uniform,
The rebel dresses in fantastic clothes.
When everybody wears fantastic clothes,
The rebel dresses soberly.

(i) What does the rebel wear when everybody puts on fantastic clothes?

(ii) Identify the poem from which the above lines has been taken.

(iii) Who has written the above lines?

(iv) Choose noun of the word 'soberly'.

(a) Sober ☐ (b) Soberness ☐

(c) Soberfull ☐ (d) Sweet ☐

(v) Choose antonym of the word 'fantastic'.

(a) Superb ☐ (b) Beautiful ☐

(c) Awesome ☐ (d) Ordinary ☐

2

When everybody is praising the sun,
The rebel remarks on the need for rain.
When everybody is greeting the rain,
The rebel regrets the absence of sun.

(i) What should happen to make the rebel like sunlight?

(ii) Suggest a different title for the poem.

(iii) When everybody greeted the rains, what did the rebel do?

(iv) The word 'rebellion' is a

(a) Noun ☐ (b) Adverb ☐

(c) Pronoun ☐ (d) Verb ☐

(v) A word that rhymes with 'absence' is

(a) substantive ☐ (b) quietness ☐

(c) presence ☐ (d) convenient ☐

Fill in the Blanks

1 Sita likes to keep ____________ hair.

2 Is it ____________ for girls to move outside their house after 9 pm?

3 One person was killed while five people were ____________ injured in the accident.

4 She ____________ stood up and vanished from the park.

Imagination Based Questions

1 Imagine a situation in which your best friend behaves like a rebel and does the opposite of what you say. How will you handle such a situation?

2 Think of some of the ways through which we can correct all the rebels and make them do right things like everyone else.

3 Would you like to be a rebel someday? Why or why not?

[Poem 3]

The Shed

Frank Flynn

Very Short Answer Type Questions

1 Who informed the poet about the presence of ghost?

2 Where did the ghost hide itself?

3 Who would probably chop off the poet's head?

Short Answer Type Questions

1 Describe the shed which the poet desperately wanted to visit.

2 What does the poet want to do about the shed?

3 Why did the poet's brother say that there was a ghost in the shed?

Long Answer Type Question

1 Do you think one should visit a place which is abandoned by others? Give reasons to support your answer. **(VBQ)**

Extract Based Questions

Directions Read the extracts given below carefully and answer the following questions.

1

There's a shed at the bottom of our garden
With a spider's web hanging across the door,
The hinges are rusty and creak in the wind.
When I'm in bed I lie and I listen,
I'll open that door one day.

(i) Who is the speaker of the above lines?

(ii) Where is the spider's web located?

(iii) Where did the poet find the shed?

(iv) Choose antonym of the word 'bottom'.

(a) Below
(b) Top
(c) Behind
(d) Between

(v) Choose synonym of the word 'creak'.

(a) Squeak
(b) Squeeze
(c) Square
(d) Press

2

There's a dusty old window around at the side
With three cracked panes of glass,
I often think there's someone staring at me
Each time that I pass,
I'll peep through that window one day.

(i) Who will peep through the window one day?

(ii) What did the poet notice about the glass panes?

(iii) What kind of perception does the poet have?

(iv) An Adjective from the above lines is

(a) peep
(b) window
(c) dusty
(d) panes

(v) A word that means 'to look at someone is'

(a) old
(b) dusty
(c) pass
(d) stare

Imagination Based Questions

1 Have you seen any building or house in your neighbourhood which is lying vacant and full of spider webs, dust etc? If yes, do you wonder why its vacant and think of going inside?

2 Elders often create a fear of unknown ghosts or animals in the minds of the children. Does this lead to curiosity more than fear? What do you think?

Chivvy

Michael Rosen

Very Short Answer Type Questions

1. Who generally gives instructions and orders to children?

2. When are children instructed to speak-up?

3. List three things that the grown-ups don't want children to do.

4. Why do parents ask their children to say 'please'?

5. What happens when children make noise?

Short Answer Type Questions

1. Do you think dragging one's feet is a bad habit? Give reasons to support your answer.

2. List any three good habits as per the poem 'Chivvy'.

3. Why are children being asked to make their own mind in the poem 'Chivvy'?

4. Do you think the title of the poem - 'Chivvy' is appropriate? Give reasons to support your answer.

5. What are three do's and don'ts for the children, according to the poem 'Chivvy'?

Long Answer Type Questions

1 Do you think it is justified to be strict with your children while teaching them good manners? Give reasons. **(VBQ)**

2 Do you think teachers and parents should teach and instruct children how to behave properly in public? Give reasons to support your answer. **(VBQ)**

Extract Based Questions

Direction *Read the extracts given below carefully and answer the following questions.*

1

Grown-ups say things like:
Speak up
Don't talk with your mouth full
Don't stare
Don't point
Don't pick your nose

(i) Who is the person being instructed in the above lines?

(ii) Why are children usually told not to stare?

(iii) What is nose-picking? Should you do it?

(iv) Choose antonym of the word 'full'.

(a) Top (b) Empty
(c) Heavy (d) Cold

(v) Choose synonym of the word 'grown-up.'

(a) Growth (b) Greed
(c) Younger (d) Adult

2

Sit up
Say please
Less noise
Shut the door behind you
Don't drag your feet
Haven't you got a hankie?
Take your hands out of your pockets

(i) Name the poem and the poet of the above lines.

(ii) What are the above lines? Who is saying them?

(iii) What do you mean by the word 'hankie'? When is it required?

(iv) The adverb of the word 'noisy' would be

(a) noisily ☐ (b) noise ☐
(c) noisyid ☐ (d) nuisance ☐

(v) A word that rhymes with 'take' is

(a) hands ☐ (b) feet ☐
(c) out ☐ (d) fake ☐

Fill in the Blanks

1 Why are you ______ your feet?

2 Go and ______ the main door behind you.

3 Don't ______ noise in the class.

4 I told you many times to ______ your hands out of your pockets.

5 He ______ me, while I was talking to my friend over phone.

Imagination Based Questions

1 Imagine a situation in which you have to make a similar list of instructions for the grown-ups. What would you write?

2 Suppose there are no adults in this world, only children around you. You think the world will be a happy place or a place full of chaos?

[Poem 5]

Trees

Shirley Bauer

Very Short Answer Type Questions

1 Where do birds build their nests?

2 What kind of parties can be organised under the trees?

3 What do mothers say about trees?

4 List three items made from trees. Answer in context of the poem 'Trees'.

Short Answer Type Questions

1 Do you think children love trees? Give reasons to support your answer.

2 Which game can be played near a tree?

3 What is the role of trees during the winter and summer seasons?

Long Answer Type Questions

1 We cut innumerable trees every year for many purposes. Do you think it is right to cut trees? Give reasons. **(VBQ)**

2 Do you think trees are helpful for human beings, animals and birds? Give reasons to support your answer. **(VBQ)**

Extract Based Questions

Directions *Read the extracts given below carefully and answer the following questions.*

1

Trees are for birds.
Trees are for children.
Trees are to make tree houses in.
Trees are to swing swings on.
Trees are for the wind to blow through.
Trees are to hide behind in 'Hide and Seek.'
Trees are to have tea parties under.
Trees are for kites to get caught in.

(i) Name the poem and its poet.

(ii) Who can make houses on trees?

(iii) Name a game that can be played behind a tree.

(iv) Find synonym for the word 'hide'.

(a) Child ☐ (b) Mother ☐
(c) Conceal ☐ (d) House ☐

(v) Choose antonym for the word 'make'.

(a) Break ☐ (b) Bird ☐
(c) Build ☐ (d) Blow ☐

2

Trees are to make cool shade in summer.
Trees are to make no shade in winter.
Trees are for apples to grow on and pears;
Trees are chop down and call, "TIMBER-R-R!"
Trees make mothers say,
"What a lovely picture to paint!"
Trees make fathers say,
"What a lot of leaves to rake this fall!"

(i) How are fruits and trees related?

(ii) What will be done to leaves which fall on the ground?

(iii) Do we need trees during the summer season? Give a reason to support your answer.

(iv) The word 'lovely' in 'lovely picture' is a

(a) Verb ☐ (b) Adjective ☐

(c) Pronoun ☐ (d) Adverb ☐

(v) A word that rhymes with 'timber' is

(a) rake ☐ (b) make ☐

(c) ginger ☐ (d) call ☐

Imagination Based Questions

1 Imagine yourself as a bird and write how does it feel to live in a house (nest) inside a tree?

2 Have you ever been on a Safari in a national park/forest? If yes, share your experience of being sorrounded by tall trees, hundreds of years old, and still serving all living beings.

[Poem 6]

Mystery of the Talking Fan

Maude Rubin

Very Short Answer Type Questions

1 Why did the fan begin to talk?

2 What does not matter to the poet in the poem 'Mystery of the Talking Fan'?

3 What makes the fan move?

4 Who oiled the fan's whirling motor?

5 What did the poet mention about the fan?

Short Answer Type Questions

1 Do you think a fan can really chatter? Give reasons to support your answer.

2 Justify the title of the poem 'Mystery of the Talking Fan'.

3 Why did the fan need oiling? Did it talk again after it was oiled?

Long Answer Type Question

1 In the last line of the poem the poet says that the fan became as still as water. What does this mean?

Extract Based Questions

Directions *Read the extracts given below carefully and answer the following questions.*

1

Once there was a talking fan —
Electrical his chatter.
I couldn't quite hear what he said
And I hope it doesn't matter

(i) What do you mean by 'a talking fan'?

(ii) Who is 'I' in the above mentioned lines?

(iii) Did the poet understand the language of the fan?

(iv) Find synonym for the word 'chatter'.

(a) Electricity ☐ (b) Air ☐
(c) Gossip ☐ (d) Hear ☐

(v) Find antonym for the word 'hope'.

(a) Issue ☐ (b) Topic ☐
(c) Read ☐ (d) Hopeless ☐

2

Because one day somebody oiled
His little whirling motor
And all the mystery was spoiled—
He ran as still as water.

(i) What happened one day in the life of the fan?

(ii) Which movement of the fan has been compared with water?

(iii) Who is 'he' in the above lines?

(iv) The word 'quickly' is a

(a) Adverb ☐ (b) Pronoun ☐
(c) Noun ☐ (d) Verb ☐

(v) A word that rhymes with 'mystery' is

(a) day ☐ (b) spoiled ☐
(c) history ☐ (d) water ☐

Imagination Based Questions

1 Imagine yourself as a fan. If you begin talking like the fan in the poem, what would you tell human beings?

2 Suppose you get a chance to become an electronic machine. Which machine would it be and why?

3 Is there any machine in your house which makes a lot of noise? Have you ever thought why do they make noise? Are they trying to say something?

Poem 7

Dad and the Cat and the Tree

Kit Wright

Very Short Answer Type Questions

1 Who was stuck on the tree initially in the poem 'Dad and the Cat and the Tree'?

2 What was advised to Dad? Did he follow it?

3 What was Plan B? Did it work?

Short Answer Type Questions

1 How does Dad land in the flower bed?

2 Do you think Dad was overconfident? Give reasons to support your answer.

3 What was Plan C? Did the father succeed this time?

4 How did the father manage to land on the tree?

Long Answer Type Questions

1 Throughout the poem we see Mum's fear and hesitations with reference to Dad and his plans. Does her fear prove right in the end? Give reasons to support your answer.

2 What do we learn from the poem 'Dad and the Cat and the Tree'? Is it right to save animals at the cost of our own lives? **(VBQ)**

Extract Based Questions

Directions *Read the extracts given below carefully and answer the following questions.*

1

This morning a cat got,
Stuck in our tree. Dad said, "Right, just,
Leave it to me." The tree was wobbly,
The tree was tall. Mum said, "For goodness'
Sake don't fall!"

(i) What did the family notice in the morning?

(ii) Who took the initiative to save the cat?

(iii) "Leave it to me." Who said this line?

(iv) The word 'tree' is a

(a) Abstract Noun ☐ (b) Proper Noun ☐

(c) Common Noun ☐ (d) Collective Noun ☐

(v) A word that rhymes with 'stuck' is

(a) truck ☐ (b) fall ☐

(c) hack ☐ (d) make ☐

2

'Fall?' scoffed Dad,
"A climber like me? Child's play, this is!
You wait and see." He got out the ladder,
From the garden shed. It slipped. He landed. In the flower bed.

(i) Who is 'he' in the above lines?

(ii) Who was instructed to 'wait and see' in the above lines?

(iii) Where was the ladder kept?

(iv) The synonym of 'scoff' is

(a) clever ☐ (b) scold ☐

(c) mock ☐ (d) cry ☐

(v) Choose antonym for the word 'child'.

(a) Father ☐ (b) Adult ☐

(c) Younger ☐ (d) Kid ☐

Imagination Based Questions

1 Imagine yourself in place of the Dad from the poem 'Dad and the Cat and the Tree.' If you found a cat or any other animal stuck in a tree, how would you save it?

____

____

____

2 Is there any particular activity that you enjoy doing with your mum and dad? Do you think that any activity can become interesting when it is done together with your family?

____

____

____

Poem 8

Meadow Surprises

Lois Brandt Phillips

Very Short Answer Type Questions

1 How should one walk on the grass?

2 Why did the butterfly unfold its drinking straws?

3 How will anyone notice a rabbit?

4 Where do ants live in the poem 'Meadow Surprises'?

5 The poet has advised us to explore burrows and nests. Where can we find these?

Short Answer Type Questions

1 How can we discover surprises in the meadows?

2 What is mentioned about a dandelion flower in the poem?

3 Why did the poet of the poem 'Meadow Surprises' advise his readers to look around and listen well?

Long Answer Type Questions

1 Should we take care of the greenery around us? Why or why not? **(VBQ)**

2 Do you think a person needs keen eyes and sharp ears to enjoy a meadow? **(VBQ)**

Extract Based Questions

Directions *Read the extracts given below carefully and answer the following questions.*

1
Meadows have surprises, You can find them if you look;
Walk softly through the velvet grass, And listen by the brook.
You may see a butterfly, Rest upon a buttercup
And unfold its drinking straws, To sip the nectar up.

(i) Where can you find wonderful things?

(ii) What is as soft as velvet?

(iii) Where do butterflies take rest?

(iv) Choose synonym of the word 'surprise'.

(a) Reveal ☐ (b) Wonder ☐

(c) Information ☐ (d) Beautiful ☐

(v) The meaning of the word 'brook' is

(a) fish ☐ (b) bird ☐

(c) a small stream ☐ (d) book ☐

2
You may scare a rabbit, Who is sitting very still;
Though at first you may not see him, When he hops you will.
A dandelion whose fuzzy head, Was golden days ago
Has turned to airy parachutes, That flutter when you blow.

(i) Who might scare the rabbit?

(ii) What happens to the golden head of the dandelions?

(iii) What do you mean by 'fuzzyhead'?

(iv) The Adverb of 'scare' is

(a) scarily ☐ (b) scared ☐

(c) scaring ☐ (d) scar ☐

(v) A word that rhymes with 'flutter' is

(a) you ☐ (b) airy ☐

(c) golden ☐ (d) butter ☐

True or False

1 A meadow is a grassland full of plants and trees and various animals and insects. ☐

2 A butterfly produces the nectare. ☐

3 Meadows offer more surprises if we look and listen well. ☐

4 The brook does not make any sound. ☐

5 A dandelion never flutters. ☐

Imagination Based Question

1 Suppose you turn into a rabbit one day. Describe the carefree life that you will enjoy hopping around in the beautiful meadows.

Poem 9

Garden Snake

Muriel L Sonne

Very Short Answer Type Questions

1 Why did the child run away in the poem 'Garden Snake'?

2 What was the advice given to the child?

3 What do the snake seen by the child generally eat?

4 What did the child tell himself?

5 Do you think all snakes are poisonous?

Short Answer Type Questions

1 "There's no mistake." What does the poet want to convey by this line?

2 How did the child's perception about snakes change?

Long Answer Type Questions

1 Do you think our assumptions are always right about certain things in life? Explain with examples. **(VBQ)**

2 Do you think the title of the poem 'Garden Snake' is appropriate? Give reasons. **(VBQ)**

3 Describe briefly the activities of the child. Answer in context of the poem 'Garden Snake.'

Extract Based Questions

Directions *Read the extracts given below carefully and answer the following questions.*

1

I saw a snake and ran away...
Some snakes are dangerous, they say;
But mother says that kind is good,
And eats up insects for his food.

(i) Who is 'I' in the above lines?

(ii) Why some snakes are dangerous?

(iii) Who eats up insects?

(iv) Choose antonym for the word 'dangerous'.

(a) Destructive ☐ (b) Damaging ☐
(c) Hostile ☐ (d) Harmless ☐

(v) Find synonym for the word 'eat'.

(a) Consume ☐ (b) Drink ☐
(c) Take ☐ (d) Walk ☐

2

So when he wiggles in the grass,
I'll stand aside and watch him pass,
And tell myself, "There's no mistake,
It's just a harmless garden snake!"

(i) Who moved in the grass?

(ii) Who was keeping an eye on the snake's movement?

(iii) What will the poet tell herself?

(iv) The word 'harmless' in the above lines is a

(a) Noun ☐ (b) Adjective ☐

(c) Verb ☐ (d) Adverb ☐

(v) The antonym of 'pass' is

(a) mass ☐ (b) near ☐

(c) fail ☐ (d) jail ☐

Imagination Based Questions

1 Would you like to keep a snake as your pet. Why or why not?

2 Imagine yourself in place of the poet. How would you react if you come across a snake in your garden?

Supplementary

[Chapter 1]

The Tiny Teacher

Very Short Answer Type Questions

1. How ants have been praised by the author?

2. How do ants talk to other ants?

3. Where do ants live?

4. What are grubs?

5. Where do the ants keep their food?

Short Answer Type Questions

1. How people have come to know about the life of ants?

2. How does a grub become a complete ant?

3. What is taught by old ants to the new ones during the training?

4. How ants can be true teachers for humans?

5. How do the worker ants take care of the grubs?

Long Answer Type Questions

1 Do the ants follow the rule of division of labour? Describe.

2 In the Lesson, it is mentioned that people have kept ants as pets? Do you think such an act is justifiable keeping in mind the various qualities and life style of ants. **(VBQ)**

True or False

1 The commonest ant is brown or red. ☐

2 An ant's life is very peaceful. ☐

3 The wedding flight of Queen ant takes place on a cool winter day. ☐

4 The greenfly is the ants' cow. ☐

5 Perfect ants come out of cocoons. ☐

Imagination Based Questions

1 The chapter mentions how some people have kept ants as pets and have watched their daily behaviour closely. What would you do if you get to keep ants as your pets?

2 Have you ever wondered how an anthill must be from the inside? Do anthills have rooms similar to human houses? Think of some of the similarities and differences.

Chapter 2

Bringing Up Kari

Dhan Gopal Mukerji

Very Short Answer Type Questions

1 Who was Kari?

2 How old was Kari when he was given to the author to take care of?

3 What is the easiest way to lead an elephant?

4 What kind of branches was Kari fond of eating?

Short Answer Type Questions

1 Where did Kari live?

2 Why did it take half an hour to sharpen the hatchet?

3 How did the author react when he found out the culprit behind the missing bananas?

4 What happened after the author scolded Kari for stealing bananas?

Long Answer Type Questions

1 How did Kari used to take a bath?

2 How did Kari save a drowning boy? Describe.

3 Attempt a character sketch of the author.

4 What can plants and animals teach us? **(VBQ)**

True or False

1 Kari saved the life of a boy.

2 The author was a good swimmer.

3 The author was happy to see Kari eating bananas.

4 Kari ate too much.

5 Kari is a fast learner.

Imagination Based Questions

1 Imagine yourself in place of the author. What would you do if you find your pet stealing something?

2 Just like Kari saved a boy from drowning, have you ever heard of any other incident where an animal saved a human's life from danger? Share your story.

[Chapter 3]

Golu Grows a Nose

Rudyard Kipling

Very Short Answer Type Questions

1. What was the difficulty with the bulgy nose?

2. Why did the ostrich, the giraffe, the hippopotamus and the baboon find Golu to be a naughty baby?

3. What did Golu ask mynah?

4. What did Golu see on the bank of the river?

5. What did the crocodile tell Golu about his dinner?

Short Answer Type Questions

1. What did Golu take along with him while going to the Limpopo river?

2. Why did the crocodile shed tears? Did the crocodile have good intentions?

3. What was the advice given by the python to Golu when he was hurt by the crocodile?

4. What did Golu do after his bumpy nose became long?

5. What was the first advantage of a long nose to Golu?

Long Answer Type Questions

1 How was Golu saved by the python?

2 What were the second and third advantages of a long nose to Golu?

3 Do you think being curious is a good thing? Apart from being curious, what should one take care of ? Is there a lesson that you can learn from the story 'Golu Grows a Nose'. **(VBQ)**

True or False

1 Long ago the elephant had no trunk. ☐
2 The ostrich was Golu's uncle. ☐
3 Golu is a clever baby. ☐
4 Golu was afraid of crocodile. ☐
5 The crocodile slipped into the water making it all creamy. ☐

Imagination Based Questions

1 Suppose your nose gets stretched like Golu's nose and turns into a trunk. What are the various things that you can do using the trunk? How would you feel?

2 If you get a chance to meet all the animals mentioned in the story 'Golu Grows a Nose', would you like to ask them few questions? If yes, what would you like to ask?

Chapter 4

Chandni

Zakir Husain

Very Short Answer Type Questions

1 With whom did Abbu Khan used to live?

2 What funny names did Abbu Khan use for his goats?

3 What did Abbu Khan do to get rid of his loneliness?

4 Who was Chandni?

5 What was Chandni informed about the hills by Abbu Khan?

Short Answer Type Questions

1 How did Abbu Khan used to treat his goats?

2 Why did the goats use to leave Abbu Khan?

3 Why Abbu Khan was unlucky in the matter of his goats?

4 Why was Chandni a winner according to a wise old bird?

Long Answer Type Questions

1 Give a description about Chandni. What kind of relation was there between her and Abbu Khan?

2 Why did Chandni want to go to the hills?

3 Do you think Chandni should have chosen the safe and protective environment offered by Abbu Khan or she did the right thing by following her dreams? Discuss with reference to the story.

True or False

1 Chandni loved the rope around her neck. ☐

2 Kalua fought the wolf bravely but was killed in the morning. ☐

3 Abbu Khan locked Chandni in the cellar. ☐

4 Chandni agreed to play with a herd of wild goats. ☐

5 The wolf was in a hurry to kill poor Chandni. ☐

Imagination Based Question

1 Imagine yourself in place of Abbu Khan, what would you have done to save your goats from disappearing in the hills?

Chapter 5

The Bear Story

Axel Munthe

Very Short Answer Type Questions

1 How strong was the bear?

2 What is the best thing that a bear likes to eat?

3 Where did the lady go on Sundays?

4 Why was the lady angry with the bear?

5 Why was the bear punished?

Short Answer Type Questions

1 What was the condition of the bear when it was found in the forest?

2 What was the bear's favourite fruit? Did he get it easily?

3 What kind of restriction was put on the bear?

4 How was it proved that the bear was a bad sailor?

5 Did the pet bear attack the lady in the forest? Why or why not?

Long Answer Type Questions

1 What kind of relation was there between the bear and other animals?

2 What did the lady see after coming back to home? What was informed to her by the cook?

True or False

1 The lady lived in an abandoned house. ☐

2 The bear loved to eat meat. ☐

3 The bear was put on the chain at night and on Sunday afternoon. ☐

4 Once the bear faced some difficulties with the beehives. ☐

Imagination Based Questions

1 What would you do if your parents gift you a bear as a pet? What are the various enjoyable things that one can do with a pet bear?

2 Suppose while passing through a forest, a bear begins to follow you. How would you react in this situation?

[Chapter 6]

A Tiger in the House

Ruskin Bond

Very Short Answer Type Questions

1 Where did Grandfather find Timothy?

2 How was Timothy fed in the initial stage?

3 Who were the companions of Timothy?

4 What was one of the favourite amusements of Timothy?

5 What was Timothy's favourite place in the house?

Short Answer Type Questions

1 How did Timothy react with the puppy initially?

2 What were Timothy's habits?

3 Where did Timothy get shifted? What did he do there?

4 Do you think that the tiger who was there in the zoo could have hurt grandfather?

Long Answer Type Questions

1 What kind of change was seen in Timothy?

2 How did grandfather react after coming to know about Timothy?

3 One should be kind towards animals. Do you agree with this statement? Why or why not? **(VBQ)**

True or False

1 Timothy was named by the author's grandfather. ☐

2 Mahmoud, the cook was responsible for feeding Timothy. ☐

3 Grandfather often quietened Timothy by smacking him across the mouth. ☐

4 Timothy died of old age. ☐

5 Timothy was transferred to a zoo in Lucknow. ☐

Imagination Based Questions

1 Imagine yourself in place of the grandfather of the story. What would you do if you find a tiger cub in the forest?

2 Do you think that animals must be allowed to live in their natural habitats and not in our homes? Share your views.

Chapter 7

An Alien Hand

Jayant Narlikar

Very Short Answer Type Questions

1 When were the two missions sent to Mars?

2 What were the names of the spacecrafts used in the Mars mission?

3 Where did Tilloo and his parents live?

4 How did Tilloo's father go to work?

5 Why was it difficult for an ordinary person to live on the surface of the planet?

6 Who lived on the surface of Mars earlier?

7 What happened after Tilloo pressed the red button?

Short Answer Type Questions

1 How did Tilloo come in the passage?

2 How was Tilloo's father able to survive at the surface?

3 Why was the control room full of excitement?

4 What was the statement given by the President?

5 What were the activities happening from the spacecraft?

Long Answer Type Questions

1 What were the views given by number One, Two and Three respectively?

2 What were the statements given by the NASA scientists in the press conference?

3 Humans are searching for life on other planets. Suppose you meet an alien one day. What would be your reaction? How would you communicate with him? Would you have a friendly attitude towards him? Why or why not? **(VBQ)**

True or False

1 Number one was in charge of social service. ☐

2 First the birds became extinct. ☐

3 Tilloo looked forward to seeing the Moon. ☐

4 The President of the Central Committee made an important statement. ☐

5 Tilloo accompanies his father to the control room. ☐

Imagination Based Questions

1 Suppose you have to live like Tilloo, beneath the surface of a planet under artificial conditions. How will it be different from our present life?

2 Imagine a spaceship lands infront of your house. Will you look into it or immediately inform the space organisations? What will you do?

Chapter 1

Articles

1. Fill in the blanks using article 'A' or 'The'.

(i) Try and eat ________ little now.

(ii) Have you ever seen ________ crocodile?

(iii) He took ________ hundred sugarcanes.

(iv) ________ python coiled himself.

(v) He saw ________ python.

2. Fill in the blanks using article (A, An, The).

(i) He discovered ________ little tiger about eighteen inches long.

(ii) He slept at night in ________ cook's quarters.

(iii) ________ tiger approached the bars.

(iv) ________ number of people had gathered to watch the reunion.

(v) Grandfather took what seemed to him ________ age to withdraw his hand from ________ cage.

3. The following sentences contain some mistakes regarding the improper use or lack of articles. Correct the sentences and rewrite them in the space provided below each sentence.

(i) I will visit an temple in a morning.

____

(ii) My father applied plans A, B and C to save a cat.

____

(iii) Are you going to watch an movie today?

____

(iv) I visited a shop to buy boots after two years.

____

(v) What the beautiful scene!

____

4. The following passage has not been edited. There is an error in each line. Find the errors and make corrections. Write the error and the correct word in the space provided. The first one has been done for you as an example.

		Incorrect	Correct
	Bachendri Pal was a first	a	the
(i)	Indian woman to reach a summit of Mount	________	________
	Everest in 1984. She became famous and in 1985,		
	she returned to Mount Everest		
(ii)	to lead a all-woman team	________	________
(iii)	to a summit.	________	________

5. Rearrange the following words/phrases to form meaningful sentences. Circle the articles in each sentence.

(i) major / the / of / are / South Indian states / producers / in / coffee / India

____

____

(ii) place / our lives / music / has / important / in / an

____

____

(iii) from God / a precious / life / is / to / gift / us

____

____

(iv) most / in / the / populated / world / China / is / country / the

____

____

(v) coastal / Koala bears / found / the / are / areas / Australia / in / the / of

____

____

6. In the following passage, one word has been omitted from each line. There is a slash(/) at the place where the word has been omitted. Mention the omitted word in the space provided. The first one has been done for you as an example.

	Lutyen's Delhi is/ area in New Delhi	an
(i)	that has been named after /leading	________
	British architect, Edwin Lutyens. He	
(ii)	was responsible for/architectural	________
(iii)	work when India was/part of	________
(iv)	/British Empire.	________

[Chapter 2]

Nouns and Pronouns

1. Write singular form of the following nouns.

(i) Desires ____________________

(ii) Clothes ____________________

(iii) Streets ____________________

(iv) Theatres ____________________

(v) Waiters ____________________

2. Make noun from the following words.

(i) Starve ____________________

(ii) Disappoint ____________________

(iii) Annoy ____________________

(iv) Interrupt ____________________

(v) Attentive ____________________

(vi) Discover ____________________

(vii) Wobbly ____________________

(viii) Good ____________________

(ix) Dirty ____________________

(x) Great ____________________

(xi) Safe ____________________

3. Identify the nouns in the following sentences.

(i) Mr Purcell owns a pet shop. ____________________

(ii) He sold cats and dogs in the shop. ____________________

(iii) Look at that little cage! ____________________

(iv) The shopkeeper slid off his stool. ____________________

(v) A white rat, perhaps. ____________________

(vi) He was found near Dehra. ____________________

(vii) Timothy is playful and naughty. ____________________

(viii) I came to live with grandfather. ____________________

(ix) About six months later he went home. ____________________

(x) A leopard in the next cage snarled. ____________________

4. Rearrange the following words / phrases to form meaningful sentences. Also circle the nouns in each sentence.

(i) has / heritage / rich / India / a / cultural

____

(ii) set out / sick / to / Little Red Riding Hood / her / immediately / see / grandmother

____

(iii) parts / many / coffee / popular / in / world / the / is / very / of

____

(iv) Mohit / and / skating / Saturday / went / on / Preeti

____

(v) Mr Nath / facts / has / Maya / about / written / some

____

5. Fill in the blanks with suitable personal pronouns from the brackets.

(i) ____________ is in-charge of the kitchen. (She, I, We)

(ii) ____________ look forward to seeing ____________ again. (We, He, You)

(iii) When will ____________ give Tony ____________ birthday present? (I, you, him, his)

(iv) How much money can ____________ give ____________? (I, me, my, your)

(v) ____________ studied in Amity University. (Him, His, He)

6. The following passage has not been edited. There is one error in each line. Find the errors and make corrections. Write the error and the correct word in the space provided. The first one has been done for you as an example.

		Incorrect	**Correct**
	Mahatma Gandhi is famously called 'Bapu'.		
	Him full name was Mohan Das Karamchand Gandhi.	Him	His
(i)	His was a great freedom	________	________
(ii)	fighter which fought against	________	________
(iii)	the British. Himself was born	________	________
(iv)	on 2nd October, 1869. Him was assassinated	________	________
	by the Hindu activist, Nathuram Godse.		

7. Fill in the blanks with suitable interrogative pronouns from the box.

Which	What	Whose	Who	Whom

(i) ____________ did the police find in the investigation?

(ii) ____________ book are you reading at the present moment?

(iii) ____________ built the Taj Mahal?

(iv) ____________ bag is this?

(v) ____________ did you have lunch with?

[Chapter 3]

Conjunctions

1. Fill in the blanks with suitable conjunctions from the box.

or, but, as, and, if, because, so that, after, when

(i) I wanted to buy the book ________________ didn't have enough money.

(ii) I did it ________________ I was very angry.

(iii) Is it a new house ________________ an old one?

(iv) Fire is both useful ________________ harmful for human beings.

(v) Mr Sharma was upset ________________ of his son's performance.

(vi) Jean could not get a job ________________ nobody would trust him.

(vii) I left home ________________ lunch.

(viii) ________________ I was a little girl, I loved to climb trees.

(ix) I left from home early ________________ I could reach office on time.

(x) Catch me ________________ you can.

2. Form single sentences using suitable conjunctions.

(i) Meena gave me a cake. I didn't eat it.

____

(ii) I visited the Grand Canyon. I go to Arizona.

____

(iii) This is the place. We stayed here last time we visited.

____

(iv) I couldn't get a seat. I came early.

____

(v) She is honest. Everyone trusts her.

____

3. Tick (✓) the correct option.

(i) I have a sister __________ is fat.

(a) it ☐ (b) who ☐

(c) she ☐ (d) her ☐

(ii) __________ I was ill, I did not write the exam.

(a) As ☐ (b) Before ☐

(c) Only ☐ (d) Though ☐

(iii) Rustam writes for pleasure ________ Sorab writes for profit.

(a) though ☐ (b) or ☐

(c) also ☐ (d) while ☐

(iv) He was tired, ________ he went to rest in the room.

(a) because ☐ (b) that ☐

(c) so ☐ (d) before ☐

(v) Keep walking ________ you see a gate.

(a) till ☐ (b) after ☐

(c) after ☐ (d) before ☐

4. Some of the sentences mentioned below have incorrect conjunctions used in them. Identify them and rewrite them properly.

(i) I could not catch the train, so I reached the station very late.

____

(ii) I respect him and he is an honest man.

____

(iii) He was guilty but he was punished.

____

(iv) I reached the clock tower, there my friend would meet me.

____

(v) You will not make mistakes and pay attention to your work.

____

5. Underline the conjunctions in the following sentences.

(i) The snowfall was heavy, so the cars moved slowly.

____

____

(ii) When Reena saw me at the restaurant, she came to join me.

____

____

(iii) The musicians delivered a rousing performance, as they had rehearsed often.

____

____

(iv) I was listening to music while you were working in the kitchen.

____

____

(v) He sells apples as well as pineapples.

____

____

Chapter 4

Adjectives

1. Fill in the blanks with the appropriate adjectives from the box.

famous	noisy	redder
unfortunate	lazy	violent
rude	precious	common
crowded	pretty	ordinary

(i) Every drop of water is ________________ .

(ii) Samrat was an ________________ horse.

(iii) His car is ________________ than mine.

(iv) George Bernard Shaw was a ________________ nineteenth century dramatist.

(v) Ramita's behaviour is very ________________ and unpredictable.

(vi) The metro station was ________________ and ________________ .

(vii) A ________________ storm uprooted the great banyan tree.

(viii) Jean told the Bishop about his ________________ story.

(ix) Sandstone is a ________________ sedimentary rock.

(x) ________________ as a picture she is!

2. Write superlative degree of the following words.

(i) Small ________________

(ii) Large ________________

(iii) Strong ________________

(iv) Strange ________________

(v) Long ________________

3. Write the comparative degree of the following words.

(i) Big ________________

(ii) Slow ________________

(iii) Small ________________

(iv) Fast ________________

(v) Hard ________________

4. Give the comparative and superlative forms of following adjectives.

	Comparative	Superlative
(i) Cold	______	______
(ii) Clean	______	______
(iii) Happy	______	______
(iv) Funny	______	______
(v) Nervous	______	______

5. Choose the correct degree of adjectives in the following sentences.

(i) The grapes taste (*sweeter/sweetest*) than the apples.

______

(ii) My dress is (*more expensive/most expensive*) than yours.

______

(iii) Rahul is the (*tallest/taller*) among all the boys.

______

(iv) This is the (*better/best*) place I have ever visited in India.

______

(v) Karan is (*more intelligent/most intelligent*) than Amit.

______

6. Fill in the blanks with the correct form of adjectives given in brackets.

(i) My room is ______ (tidy) than yours.
(ii) Armymen are usually ______ (courageous) than civilians.
(iii) Natraj is the ______ (strong) boy in his class.
(iv) Prithvi Raj Chauhan was the ______ (last) Rajput King to rule over Delhi.
(v) He thinks he is ______ (good) and ______ (intelligent) than others.
(vi) The question paper was ______ (difficult) than I had expected.
(vii) July and August are the ______ (wet) months of the year.
(viii) Your dress is lovely. But mine is ______ (lovely).
(ix) The Times of India is the ______ (popular) newspaper in Mumbai.
(x) Truth is ______ (strange) than fiction.

7. Use a suitable adjective to describe each of the following nouns.

(i) A ______ blow.
(ii) A ______ flower.
(iii) A ______ king.
(iv) A ______ child.
(v) A ______ city.
(vi) A ______ street.
(vii) An ______ artist.
(viii) A ______ lion.
(ix) An ______ novel.
(x) A ______ incident.

Prepositions

1. Fill in the blanks with suitable prepositions from the box.

between	for	at
of	in	to

Mount Abu, which is the only hill station *(i)* __________ Rajasthan, is very popular *(ii)* __________ that region. According *(iii)* __________ the legend, it was the home *(iv)* __________ Saint Vashishta who created the four powerful Rajput tribes. Maharaj *(v)* __________ Sirohi had given it on rent *(vi)* __________ the British Government, who used it as the headquarters *(vii)* __________ the residence *(viii)* __________ Rajputana. It is situated *(ix)* __________ the Nakki lake. It is known as a place that increases joy.

2. The following sentences are jumbled. Rearrange them to make them meaningful sentences. Also, underline the prepositions in each sentence.

(i) Shikha / read / loves / to

____

(ii) Sharan / well / jumped / into / the

____

(iii) Kerala / live / my / grandparents / in

____

(iv) damaged / it / car / her / Romita / by / against / hitting / a / wall

____

(v) old people / we / a feeling / should / of / for / acceptability / have

____

3. In the following passage one word has been omitted from each line. There is a slash (/) at the place where the word has been omitted. Mention the omitted word in the space provided. The first one has been done for you as an example.

		Before	**Missing**	**After**
	The real needs/young children	needs	of	young
(i)	are quite different. They need/develop	______	______	______
(ii)	initiative and find out things/themselves.	______	______	______
	Television provides answers easily.			
(iii)	Children need/acquire the fundamental	______	______	______
(iv)	skills/communication. Television retards verbal development because the child is silent while watching it.	______	______	______

4. Fill in the blanks with suitable prepositions from the brackets.

(i) A Bishop was moved ________ (*in/on*) seeing his pitiable condition.

(ii) ________ (*in/on*) this day, a parade takes place ________ (*at/in*) Rajpath, ________ (*in/into*) the presence ________ (*of/for*) the President ________ (*to/of*) India.

(iii) The palace is a five-storey structure ________ (*on/in*) the form ________ (*to/of*) a pyramid.

(iv) The architectural design of Hawa Mahal is a perfect example ________ (*of/with*) the fusion ________ (*of/with*) Hindu Rajput and Muslim architecture.

(v) I slept ________ (*until/till*) 10 o' clock ________ (*on/in*) the morning.

(vi) Have you killed the dog ________ (*by/with*) a spade?

(vii) It took ________ (*about/between*) one hour ________ (*for/of*) sixty fire-fighters ________ (*to/on*) extinguish the fire.

(viii) A fire ________ (*at/in*) a residential complex has left twenty people dead.

(ix) What do you think ________ (*about/under*) the talking fan?

(x) Having visited many cities ________ (*on/in*) India, he has knowledge ________ (*about/over*) them.

5. The following passage has not been edited. There is one error in each line. Find the errors and make corrections. Write the error and the correct word in the space provided. The first one has been done for you as an example.

		Incorrect	**Correct**
	Owls spend most about their	about	of
(i)	time of the dark and have an	________	________
(ii)	acute sense on hearing. They	________	________
(iii)	can detect their prey just with	________	________
(iv)	hearing them move about	________	________
	complete darkness. Owls have two		
(v)	ears, one in either side	________	________
(vi)	on the head.	________	________

6 Some words always take a specific preposition after them when they are used in a sentence. Give the prepositions that follow the words given below. Also, make sentences with the phrases formed.

(i) According ________ ________________

(ii) Result ________ ________________

(iii) Comparison ________ ________________

(iv) Aptitude ________ ________________

(v) Interested ________ ________________

(vi) Busy ________ ________________

(vii) Protect ________ ________________

(viii) Increase ________ ________________

(ix) Comment ________ ________________

(x) Disagree ________ ________________

Tenses

1. Change the following sentences into future tense.

(i) The children used to ride on his back.

(ii) He roamed freely during the day.

(iii) He ate the same food as the dogs.

(iv) The lady visited her sister.

(v) She did not want him to come with her.

2. The following passage has not been edited. There is one error in each line. Find the errors and make corrections. Write the error and the correct word in the space provided. The first one has been done for you as an example.

		Incorrect	Correct
	It has been rightly say that the	say	said
(i)	choice of books are as important as the		
(ii)	choice of friends. Books that is selected		
(iii)	is friends for a		
(iv)	life time. I known that		
(v)	it is not possible to reading all the books from a particular subject.		
(vi)	The worst thing are to		
(vii)	reading the better books on a subject.		

3. The following sentences are jumbled. Rearrange them to make them meaningful. Also, identify their tense.

(i) Hindi / she / story / translate / will / the / to

(ii) Please / speak / class / in / in / the / English

(iii) Food / he / money / does / buy / not / have / to / any

(iv) Does / not / Maya / be / Nishad / friendly / Mr Nath / want / to / with / and

____

(v) Offered / they / discount / us / a / heavy / the / car / new / on

____

4. Fill in the blanks by using the correct form of tenses of the word given in the brackets.

(i) Tony and Nick __________ (score) six baskets each.

(ii) Holi is __________ (celebrate) in various ways all over the country.

(iii) On Sunday, Tony __________ (go) to Nick's house to __________ (play) basketball.

(iv) When I __________ (reach) her house, I __________ (surprise) to see her __________ (crouch) on the ground.

(v) She had been __________ (hide) something.

(vi) Srinagar is often __________ (refer) to as 'Paradise on Earth.'

(vii) After the game, the children __________ (go) inside to have food.

(viii) I'd like to __________ (reserve) a table, please.

(ix) The shed __________ (damage) during the storm.

(x) During Holi, balloons are also __________ (fill) with coloured water and __________ (spurt) onto people.

5. Fill in the blanks with the correct words from the box.

was, were, is, am, are, have, has, had

(i) __________ you ever wondered how difficult it is for a poor person to earn his daily bread?

(ii) Srinagar __________ famous for its handicrafts and dry fruits.

(iii) Parrots __________ of many kinds.

(iv) Kashmir __________ called the Switzerland of India.

(v) His life __________ a living hell.

(vi) I __________ going to make a pizza.

(vii) This __________ not a child's play.

(viii) Oh! __________ it?

(ix) Maya and Nishad __________ brother and sister.

(x) Aalia __________ finished her homework.

(xi) They __________ not interested in the subject.

6. Listed below are the past form of a few words. Write down the present form of these words in the space given.

(i) Wrote __________

(ii) Arose __________

(iii) Forgave __________

(iv) Withdrew __________

(v) Shrank __________

(vi) Forbade __________

Verbs

1. Pick out the verbs in the following sentences.

(i) He lived all alone except for a few goats. ____________

(ii) They love their freedom. ____________

(iii) Why do you want to leave me? ____________

(iv) Let me go to the hills. ____________

(v) He seemed in no hurry. ____________

2. Fill in the blanks with appropriate forms of the word given in brackets.

(i) The old man is ____________ the ground in front of his hut since morning. (dig)

(ii) I will ____________ the king and his kingdom as his most faithful servant. (serve)

(iii) If you had not ____________ his wounds, he would have died without having made peace with you. (dress)

(iv) The king ____________ fresh water and food for the soldiers wounded in the war. (bring)

(v) The king ____________ outside the hut, looking everywhere for the hermit. (go)

3. The following passage has not been edited. There is one error in each line. Find the errors and make corrections. Write the error and the correct word in the space provided. The first one has been done for you as an example.

		Incorrect	**Correct**
	It is bad to has food stuck	has	have
	between your teeth for a long		
(i)	time. This is because food attract germs	________	________
(ii)	and germs produces acid; this	________	________
(iii)	hurt your teeth and gums. Flossing	________	________
(iv)	helped to remove the food that	________	________
(v)	gets stick between your teeth. This	________	________
(vi)	explains how flossing helping to	________	________
(vii)	keeping your mouth healthy, but	________	________
(viii)	some doctors say that floss can	________	________
(ix)	also been good for your heart.	________	________

4. In the following passages, one word has been omitted from each line. There is a slash (/) at the place where the word has been omitted. Mention the omitted word in the space provided along with words that come before and after it. The first one has been done for you as an example.

A.	**Before**	**Missing**	**After**
Shama /loved by all the	Shama	was	loved
(i) people of his village. He/an intelligent boy who	______	______	______
solved everybody's problems			
(ii) in a minute. He/alone in his small house. But	______	______	______
(iii) everybody/care of him.	______	______	______

B.	**Before**	**Missing**	**After**
The Taj Mahal/made up of	Mahal	is	made
(i) white marble. It/eight sides	______	______	______
(ii) and more open arches. There/an open corridor	______	______	______
just inside the outer walls. From this			
(iii) corridor, the visitor/through the carved	______	______	______
marble that screens a central room.			

5. Rearrange the following sentences to make them meaningful sentences. Also, underline the verbs in each sentence.

(i) coming / are / school / you / tomorrow / to / ?

____

(ii) we / deal / fantastic / signed / the / !

____

(iii) seen / he / them / never / has

____

(iv) forest / wood / woodcutter / was / the / chopping / the / in

____

(v) near / see / when / know / signs / you / these / winter / that / is / you

____

6. Use the verbs listed in the box to fill in the blanks.

play, left, finished, tries, drank, completed
scored, get, want, work, bought, prepared

(i) Sita, Madan, Seema and Isha ________ for Patna.
(ii) She ________ her test paper and ________ the class.
(iii) She ________ well for the examination. So, she ________ maximum marks in all the subjects.
(iv) They ________ their homework. Then, they ________ the room to ________ outside.
(v) I ________ a pair of shoes, three frocks and two skirts.
(vi) The old man ________ ten apples, two oranges and five mangoes.
(vii) The old man, being a farmer used to ________ in the fields.
(viii) Tilloo managed to ________ hold of his security card.
(ix) He ________ three tricks, all in vain.
(x) After arriving home, I ________ a glass of water.

Chapter 8

Adverbs

1. Pick out the adverbs in the following sentences.

(i) How often have you been told not to go that way?

(ii) Tilloo's father went everyday for work.

(iii) Tilloo's father was greatly enjoying a siesta at home.

(iv) His mother got rarely angry.

(v) The conference room in the Central Bureau was so quiet.

2. Fill in the blanks with the right word from the brackets. Also, identify the adverbs and adjectives.

(i) Sita likes to keep ____________ hair. (*long/lengthy*)

(ii) Is it ____________ for girls to move outside their house after 9 pm? (*safely/safe*)

(iii) One person was killed while five people were ____________ injured in the accident. (*severely/severe*)

(iv) She ____________ stood up and vanished from the park.(*sudden/suddenly*)

(v) Rajiv ____________ takes a cab to reach his office. (*usual/usually*)

3. Change the following words into adverb using 'ly and ily'.

(i) Rapid ____________

(ii) Prompt ____________

(iii) Luck ____________

(iv) Perfect ____________

(v) Wise ____________

4. Arrange the following words into two categories adjectives and adverbs.

lively	possibly	poor	wicked	mighty
nearly	costly	partly	suddenly	foul

Adverbs ____________

Adjectives ____________

5. Rearrange the following words/phrases to form meaningful sentences. Also, underline the adverbs in each sentence.

(i) Kanika / always / was / very / in / studies / bad

____

(ii) the / at / both / atmosphere / is / cold / these / places / very

____

(iii) carefree / some of / recall / I / can / moments / my

____

(iv) the / abruptly / bus / stopped

____

(v) disconnected / gets / after / soon / line / the

____

6. Fill in the blanks with suitable adverbs from the box.

already	ago	quietly
commonly	only	sadly
loudly	continuously	again
happily	immediately	sorrowfully

(i) Fire is __________ used to generate electricity and cook food.

(ii) My parents__________ rushed to the hospital.

(iii) I __________ listened to the lecture.

(iv) He was __________ dressed all in black.

(v) I __________ shared the good news with my friends.

(vi) This incident happened a long, long time__________.

(vii) Try, try, try __________ till you succeed.

(viii) I have __________ completed my project.

(ix) I take the metro __________ when I miss my bus.

(x) Every year tourists from all over the world __________ come to see Srinagar's everlasting beauty.

7. Rewrite the sentences using the adverbs/adverb phrases given in the brackets.

(i) The plane has taken off. (just)

____

(ii) Be prepared for the worst. (always)

____

(iii) Is the drawing room big? (enough)

____

(iv) Many tradesmen came to the Eid fair. (far and wide)

____

(v) Simi played the guitar. (skilfully)

____

Chapter 9

Modals

1. Fill in the blanks with suitable modals.

(i) He __________ take them out for grazing during the day.

(ii) Abbu Khan __________ not solve the mystery.

(iii) He loved Chandni and __________ narrate to her stories.

(iv) I __________ fight the wolf.

(v) I __________ put up a good fight.

2. Fill in the blanks with appropriate modals from the box.

shall	would	should
can	could	will
might	must	may

(i) __________ you guess my father's name?

(ii) Ram spent all his money. Therefore, he __________ not buy a new pen and pencil.

(iii) We __________ value and preserve our heritage.

(iv) I never dreamt as a child that I __________ become a millionaire one day.

(v) Look out of the window a minute, __________ you?

(vi) We __________ overcome some day!

(vii) Don't you think that I __________ have done it.

(viii) __________ I come in, Ma'am? Yes, you __________come in.

(ix) We __________ exercise regularly.

(x) Where there is a __________ ,there is a way.

3. Rearrange the following jumbled sentences in a way so as to make them meaningful sentences. Also, underline the modals in each sentence.

(i) strike / opportunity / the / wait / I / to / right / for / will

____

(ii) not / children / below / of / age / the / must / drive / eighteen / years

____

(iii) frightening / remember / I / can / moments / also / my

____

(iv) to / you / and / drink / would / like / what / ?

____

(v) could / hear / we / music / sound / of / the

____

(vi) damp / small / can / fire / be / put / a / blanket / out / with / a

____

4. The following passages have not been edited. There is one error in each line. Find the errors and make corrections. Write the error and the correct word in the space provided. The first one has been done for you as an example.

A.

		Incorrect	**Correct**
	Plastic bags are not be used	are	should
(i)	because they should cause much pollution. They never disintegrate with time.	______	______
(ii)	They should block a sewage	______	______
(iii)	pipe but that might make things even worse.	______	______

B.

		Incorrect	**Correct**
	Water is an essential component by life. There is shortage of water in many regions of our country.		
(i)	All of us must to understand the importance of water. We	______	______
(ii)	could not waste water.	______	______
(iii)	We would promote water conservation.	______	______

5. Tick (✓) the correct option.

(i) You ________ tell me the truth.

(a) should ☐ (b) could ☐

(c) would ☐ (d) must ☐

(ii) I ________ be so glad when the examinations are over.

(a) will ☐ (b) would ☐

(c) could ☐ (d) shall ☐

(iii) After the art competition, I realised that I ________ paint well.

(a) should ☐ (b) could ☐

(c) would ☐ (d) must ☐

(iv) ________ you please answer my questions?

(a) Should ☐ (b) Could ☐

(c) Will ☐ (d) Must ☐

(v) ________ you prefer to study in a boarding school?

(a) Would ☐ (b) Could ☐

(c) Should ☐ (d) Will ☐

Chapter 10

Determiners

1. Underline the determiners in the following sentences.

(i) This is a letter from my grandmother.

(ii) That is my dog Tipsy.

(iii) Those houses are for sale.

(iv) These dresses are so beautiful.

(v) How many biscuits do you want?

(vi) Some people are very clever.

(vii) There are few sweets left in the box.

(viii) There is a large amount of information on the internet.

(ix) Raina stood first in her class.

(x) All that glitters is not gold.

2. Fill in the blanks with the appropriate words from the box.

this	that	these	those

(i) Come ________ way, please.

(ii) ________ flowers are so beautiful!

(iii) ________ book is mine and ________ book is yours.

(iv) ________ kids play on the street everyday.

(v) ________ is my son, Ibrahim.

3. Complete the paragraph using correct words from the box.

few	many	most	a few

India is a popular tourist destination. There are ***(i)*** ________ entry points to India and ***(ii)*** ________ foreigners land up in Delhi at the main bazaar. The main bazaar is always packed with foreigners.

4. The following passage has not been edited. There is one error in each line. Find the errors and make corrections. Write the error and the correct word in the space provided. The first one has been done for you as an example.

		Incorrect	**Correct**
	I work with much other people in a big office.	much	many
(i)	Even winter, I fly to Goa and sit on the beach. I like	________	________
(ii)	to watch every the latest movies at the cinema hall near my house. I like to play tennis on Sunday mornings. My family goes	________	________
(iii)	for shopping in the super market many Saturday.	________	________

Chapter 11

Sentences

1. Divide each of the following sentences into subject and predicate.

(i) She did not go to Malaysia.

Subject ____________ Predicate ____________

(ii) Ramalal brought the food from the market.

Subject ____________ Predicate ____________

(iii) Karan didn't eat vegetables last night.

Subject ____________ Predicate ____________

(iv) My friend writes short stories.

Subject ____________ Predicate ____________

(v) Ramya did not sing well.

Subject ____________ Predicate ____________

2. Change the following sentences into negative.

(i) He will remember you.

____

(ii) Mary is very intelligent girl.

____

(iii) They were sad when he moved away.

____

(iv) I could not catch the train.

____

(v) Her performance was very good.

____

3. The following sentences are jumbled. Rearrange them to make them meaningful.

(i) the / Titanic / ship / sank / unsinkable / on / maiden / its / voyage

____

(ii) he / London / yesterday / left / for

____

(iii) Arjun / capable / of / is / eating / bananas / 24

____

(iv) she / good / of / her / class / student / was / a

____

(v) is the / consume / carbon dioxide / that plants / food

____

4. Change the following sentences into interrogative sentences.

(i) He goes to office at 9 o'clock.

____

(ii) She speaks English fluently.

____

(iii) He calls his mother everyday.

____

(iv) They have promised to pay higher wages.

____

(v) Kanishka doesn't like to dance.

____

5. The following passage has not been edited. There is one error in each line. Find the errors and make corrections. Write the error and the correct word in the space provided. The first one has been done for you as an example.

		Incorrect	**Correct**
	Have you ever wonder why	wonder	wondered
(i)	certain children bubble in energy?	________	________
	This energy is reflected in their		
(ii)	enthusiasm to learning and	________	________
(iii)	excelling at new things. So, super active	________	________
	kids score on two counts		
(iv)	over there counterparts in	________	________
(v)	Adequate exposure to sunlight but adequate	________	________
	intake of Vitamin D.		
(vi)	Moreover, insufficient Vitamin D is	________	________
(vii)	a strong guard for depression.	________	________

6. Fill in the Blanks with a suitable subject.

(i) ____________ has been following me.

(ii) ____________ am not at all tired.

(iii) ____________ revolve around the Sun.

(iv) ____________ is a smart, young man.

(v) ____________ is the first day of the week.

Chapter 12

Active-Passive Voice

1. Rewrite the following sentences into passive voice.

(i) Mohan bought a pair of boots from the showroom.

(ii) Mr Gessler pressed a finger on the boots.

(iii) The police caught the thief from the railway station.

(iv) I visited the shop to place an order.

(v) The cobbler mended my shoes in 10 minutes.

2. Change the following sentences into active voice.

(i) Vita-Wonk was invented by Mr Wonka.

(ii) Many countries were visited by him.

(iii) By whom were you taught to paint?

(iv) The video was posted on Facebook by an Oompa-Loompa volunteer.

(v) She was given four drops of liquid by Asha.

(vi) The city was completely destroyed by the flood.

(vii) Oranges and apples were eaten by Rajesh.

(viii) I was given a chocolate by my teacher.

(ix) The project will be completed before the deadline.

(x) Once in a month, this temple is visited by my mother.

3. Some sentences have been given below. Identify whether they are in the active or in the passive voice.

(i) Everybody liked him.

(ii) The rat was killed by the cat.

(iii) I see a lonely road.

(iv) The file was brought by the peon.

(v) Tasman discovered Australia.

(vi) I expect some good news.

(vii) The mongoose challenged the snake.

(viii) A chocolate is eaten by Madhumita.

(ix) Has she written the assignment?

(x) I have seen a shooting star.

4. The following passage has not been edited. There is one error in each line. Find the errors and make corrections. Write the error and the correct word in the space provided. The first one has been done for you as an example.

		Incorrect	**Correct**
	A bank clerk is jilted by his	is	was
	girlfriend. The only thing left to do		
(i)	was to kill himself. He stolen a car	________	________
(ii)	with the idea of crashing it, but the car break down.	________	________
(iii)	He steal another one, but it was	________	________
(iv)	too slow and he dent its bumper	________	________
(v)	when he crash the car into a tree.	________	________
(vi)	The police arrived and charge the man with auto theft.	________	________

5. Put the verb in the correct form according to the voice of the sentences.

(i) A sandwich is ____________ (make) by Richa.

(ii) An old man ____________ (answer) the door.

(iii) Mrs Pant ____________ (teach) us German.

(iv) Nishant ____________ (hand) her the letter.

(v) The book fair ____________ (inaugurate) by the Mayor.

(vi) Will the piano ____________ (play) by Alice?

(vii) The vase ____________ (break) by me yesterday.

(viii) The prizes have ____________ (collect) by the winners.

(ix) Ice-cream ____________ (make) from milk.

(x) A new building ____________ (construct) by Gaur Developers.

Chapter 13

Direct and Indirect Speech

1. Change the following sentences into indirect speech.

(i) My teacher says, "Fire is the result of a chemical reaction."

(ii) "Do not play with electrical appliances", my mother advises.

(iii) A journalist said, "The fire fighters have brought the fire under control."

(iv) "I burnt my hand while cooking food in the kitchen", Priya said.

(v) "Can you help people suffering from burns"? asks Sanjeev.

(vi) The king said to the hermit, "Let me work in your place."

(vii) The hermit said, "You (king) have already been answered."

(viii) "Forgive me !" said the bearded man.

(ix) The servant said, "My master is busy in his work."

(x) He said to me, "I don't trust you."

2. The following sentences are written in direct speech. They contain some errors related to punctuation. Correct the sentences by putting punctuation marks at the appropriate places.

(i) What a lovely weather outside she remarked.

(ii) My mother said you'll break your neck.

(iii) No cake for you said the waiter.

(iv) What a beautiful piece he said.

(v) I murmured oh I am sorry.

(vi) The old man said lets sprinkle the ashes.

3. Fill in the blanks.

(i) Direct Speech: He says, "I am glad to be here today."
Indirect Speech: He says that __________ was glad to be there __________.

(ii) Direct Speech : I said to my friend, "Please, lend me your book."
Indirect Speech: I __________ my friend to lend me his book.

(iii) Direct Speech: Mrinal said to me, "Kanishka has told a lie."
Indirect Speech: Mrinal told me __________ Kanishka had told a lie.

(iv) Direct Speech: I said, "Rani will sing a song."
Indirect Speech: I said that Rani __________ sing a song.

(v) Direct Speech: Hina said, "Good morning to you all."
Indirect Speech: Hina __________ them all good morning.

(vi) Indirect Speech: Rahul asked me what I was doing there.
Direct Speech: Rahul said to me, "what __________ you doing __________?"

(vii) Indirect Speech: Piya said that she could not do so.
Direct Speech: Piya said, "I __________ do so?"

(viii) Direct Speech: Vidushi said to Abhinav, "why don't you listen to me?"
Indirect Speech: Vidushi asked Abhinav why __________ __________ listen to __________.

Worksheet 1

(Based on Whole Grammar Content)

Directions *The following passages have not been edited. There is one error in each line. Find the errors and make corrections. Write the incorrect and the correct word in the space provided.*

1 England has long been famous for her dramatist, (a)
the greatest of who was William Shakespeare. (b)
It is hard to find the educated man in the (c)
English speaking world whom has not (d)
heard for his name. The actor and playwright (e)
Born more than 400 years ago had become not (f)
only for Englishman but for the whole world (g)
the chief symbol for British culture.

2 Summer always spells magic. That is the time. (a)
when schools closed their gates & loved (b)
ones-cousins, uncles or aunts, descend (c)
in the spacious family home. (d)
The house are big enough. (e)

3 You regret to bring this to your notice. (a)
The very poor condition of roads on their area. (b)
I hope you contact the PWD to get (c)
themselves repaired immediately. If you (d)
need help, myself am ready. (e)

4 A weary traveller stopped at an Bedouin and (a)
asked for food and shelter for an night without (b)
any delay.
A man killed a chicken and handled it to his wife (c)
for an guest's dinner. As the woman stirred the meat (d)
in the
copper cooking pot, she smelled at a rich steam (e)
coming out

		Incorrect	Correct
5 The passengers were waiting at the			
station when five policemen rushing	(a)		
into difference compartments of a			
train. After some times one of them	(b)		
comes out with two young men	(c)		
and soon the other policemen joined her.	(d)		

Worksheet 2

(Based on Whole Grammar Content)

Directions *In the passages that follow, one word has been omitted from each line. There is a slash (/) at the place where the word has been omitted. Mention the omitted word in the space provided.*

		Before	Missing	After
1 Jean could not get/job as nobody would	(a)			
trust/. Consequently his	(b)			
life/a living hell. A Bishop was	(c)			
moved/seeing his pitiable condition. The	(d)			
Bishop let him into his house/asked him the	(e)			
reason of his being so dejected. Jean told				
him/unfortunate story.	(f)			
2 Mount Abu which/the only hill station	(a)			
of Rajasthan, is very popular in/region.	(b)			
According to the legend it/the home	(c)			
of Saint Vashishta/created the four powerful	(d)			
Rajput tribes. Maharaj of Sirohi/it on rent to	(e)			
the British Government who/it as the headquarters for the	(f)			
Resident of Rajputana. It/situated at the Nakki lake. It	(g)			
is known as/place that increases joy.	(h)			
3 Mathematics is/old as civilisation itself and	(a)			
is one/the most	(b)			
useful/fascinating branches of human knowledge.	(c)			
It contains/topics of study and as such,	(d)			
it/difficult to define the term 'mathematics'	(e)			
which/from a Greek word meaning 'inclined to learn'.	(f)			

4 There/various entry points (a)
to India/most foreigners (b)
land/Delhi and (c)
a/the main bazaar, is India's (d)
The main bazaar is/packed foreigners. (e)

5 I went to my friend last week/9 am. (a)
Actually, I wanted his scooter/a day. (b)
I was shocked/he politely refused to oblidge me. (c)
Perhaps, I/mistaken in assessing what time friendship (d)
It/a lesson in my life and I was supposed to learn. (e)

Worksheet 3

(Based on Whole Grammar Content)

Directions *Change the following sentences into Negative.*

1 They have not refused the invitation.

2 You should always speak the truth.

3 He sometimes calls his mother.

4 We must love one another.

5 My friend is always present.

6 All must submit to destiny.

7 Ritu's performance was good.

8 He has left the village forever.

9 As soon as I arrived, it began to rain.

10 The contractor has many clients.

Directions *Change the following sentences into Affirmative.*

11 She did not play anything but cricket.

12 Karan got not more than 50% marks in English.

13 Kashika is not very bad at cooking.

14 Ramen is not only junk but also full of fat.

15 Ramalal is not less strong than Hasan.

16 Sanjeeda will not come here again.

17 None but mother loves her child.

18 Ramya is so weak that she cannot walk.

19 Mahajan was not a bad boy.

20 No other city in India is as big as Mumbai.

Directions *Form single sentences. Make suitable changes wherever required.*

21 Sita gave me a pastry.
I didn't eat it.

22 I visit the Grand Canyon.
I go to Switzerland.

23 This is the home.
We stayed last time we visited.

24 I couldn't get a seat.
I came early.

25 Pay attention to your work.
You will not make mistakes.

26 The dancers delivered a rousing performance.
They had rehearsed often.

27 He is honest.
Everyone trusts her.

28 The snowfall was heavy.
The bike moved slowly.

29 I reached the clock tower.
My friend would meet me there.

30 Rita saw me at the movie.
She came to join me.

Writing

[Chapter 1]

Notice Writing

Sample Notice

You are the Head Boy of your school. Write a notice informing all the students of your school about the holiday on the occasion of Id-ul-Zuha on 25th September, 20XX.

HAPPY SCHOOL

DARYAGANJ

NOTICE

17th September, 20XX

Holiday

This is to inform all the students that the school will remain closed on 25th September, 20XX (Friday) on the occasion of Id-ul-Zuha. The school will reopen on 28th September, 20XX (Monday) and the timings of the school will remain the same.

Kabir

1. Name of the institution in capital letters.
2. The word 'NOTICE is written in capital letters
3. Date on which the notice is issued towards the left.
4. Heading of the Notice.
5. Content of the Notice (what, when and where)
6. Name and designation of the person writing the notice.

Points to be kept in mind while writing a Notice

- The entire content of the Notice should be in a box.
- At the top, write the name of the issuing authority in capital letters.
- Date of issue should be mentioned on the left hand side only.
- Mention relevant/eye-catching caption.
- Language of the content should be simple, correct and clear.
- It is written in the third person. Don't use 'I', 'you'.

PRACTICE Questions

1 You are Sumit Agarwal, a seventh grade student of Ramakrishna Public School. You have lost your swimming kit in the school lobby. Draft a notice to be put up on the school notice board mentioning all the relevant details including the reward to be given to the finder. Put your notice in a box in 50 words.

2 As the School Captain of your school, you have to put up a notice informing all the students about the special screening of the movie 'Frozen' in the school auditorium. Draft a notice informing students about the same by giving all the relevant details in 50 words.

3 As Smriti Bansal of KMC School, you have to write a notice informing the students about an upcoming school tour to Jim Corbett Park to be held in the first week of August.Write a notice about the same mentioning all the relevant details like cost of the trip, lodging, transport etc in 50 words.

4 Your school is going to celebrate English Literary Fest soon. As Mukta Ahuja, Head of English Club, draft a notice inviting articles, speech, poems, etc from the students for the same. Draft a notice in 50 words giving relevant details.

5 You are Naman Ahuja, Cultural Secretary, Ramjas School. Write a notice informing the students about the auditions for the 'School Rock Band,' to be held on 25th October. Mention all the necessary details in 50 words.

6 You are Rashi Agarwal, Head Girl, Ramjas School. Your school is inviting world famous author Ruskin Bond. Draft a notice informing the students about this interactive session encouraging them to exchange views and ask questions.

7 As Head Prefect of your school you have to write a notice informing all the prefects about a school meeting to be organised on the issue of maintaining cleanliness in the school premises. Write the notice for the same giving all relevant details in 50 words.

8 You were travelling in a bus going to Delhi. On the way, you spotted a bag containing money and papers forgotten by a co-passenger. It has no name. Draft a notice to be published in the newspaper so as to locate its owner. You are Rajni Sharma, a resident of Delhi. Give all the details and put the notice in a box in 50 words.

9 You are Rajat Chawla, President, Defence Colony housing society. Write a notice urging the residents to generously donate for the flood victims of Nepal in the flood relief camp to be organised by the housing society. Put the notice in a box with all the relevant details in 50 words.

10 As the Branch Manager of World Tours Private Ltd, you want to draft a notice informing general public about the change in the address of your head office due to renovation. Draft the notice in 50 words.

Chapter 2

Message Writing

Sample Message

☑ *You are Amit. Your father's friend, Mr Ashok Walia called to speak to your father. Mr Walia tells you to inform your father that the party in the evening is cancelled. Write a message regarding the same and put it in a box.*

(1) Title
(2) Date on which the message is written.
(3) Name of the person to whom the message is meant.
(4) Content of the message
(5) Name of the person writing the message.

MESSAGE

18th September, 20XX

Dear Father,

Uncle (Mr Ashok Walia) called up in your absence to inform you that the party scheduled in the evening today has been cancelled due to some unavoidable circumstances. Please call him once you read this message. He can be reached on 97XXX-63XXX.

Amit

Points to be kept in mind while writing a Message

- Remember to mention who called, why, who to contact and any other essential detail in the message.
- The message should be written in simple and clear language.
- It should not be in more than 50 words.
- Always put the message in the box.

PRACTICE Questions

1 You are Radha. Your brother Raghav's friend Anil, called up to talk to him, but since he was not at home you took the message for him. Anil asked you to inform Raghav about the school practice session of cricket to be held tomorrow. Also, he has to bring ₹ 500 for the cricket kit. As you have to leave for your dance class, you decide to leave a message. Write the message in 50 words and put it in a box.

2 Read the following notes from the notepad of Ms Mina Bindra, Chairperson of Ramjas School, Delhi. She asks her assistant to draft a message on her behalf for Ms Shymala Agarwal, the Vice-Principal of the school. Using the information from the notepad. Draft a message in not more than 50 words.

- Attend urgent meeting
- Meeting in School Auditorium at 11.30 am today
- Agenda : Maintenance of school discipline and prevention of ragging
- Inform all concerned incharges about it
- Make report of the meeting

3 You are Anita. You have an appointment with your cousin Raj to see a football match at 3.00 pm at National Stadium. But you have to take your sister to her dance classes, so you won't be able to meet your cousin for the match. Before leaving you decide to leave a message for your cousin informing him about the same and apologising for not being able to make it. Draft a message in not more than 50 words.

4 You receive a phone call from your mother's friend, Mrs Raksha in her absence and have the following conversation with the speaker. Write a message in not more than 50 words, for your mother as you have to go for your coaching classes. Put the message in a box.

Mrs Raksha	:	Hello. Is this 25258634?
Smriti	:	Yes. May I know who's calling?
Mrs Raksha	:	I am Mrs Raksha. Can I talk to Sushila?
Smriti	:	I am afraid. Mother is not at home. Do you have any message for her?
Mrs Raksha	:	Yes. Please tell her that the shopping programme fixed for tomorrow has been postponed as one of our friends Mrs Shalini is not well. I would inform her about the new plan as soon as it is made.
Smriti	:	Ok aunty, I will inform her.
Mrs Raksha	:	Thanks and take care.

5 You are Nisha. You attended a call on behalf of your sister Rohini. Her friend Astha has called up and you noted down the following points. Draft a message in not more than 50 words.

Astha's call : Dance Audition tomorrow at 11:30 am-In School Auditorium-bring your dance costume-don't be late.

6 The following is a telephonic conversation between Mr Ashutosh, a businessman and his client's Manager Mr Gupta. His client Mr Sharma is not available, so Mr Ashutosh leaves a message for him with Mr Gupta. Write the message in 50 words.

Mr Ashutosh	:	Hello. Can I talk to Mr Sharma?
Mr Gupta	:	I am afraid he is not here. Can I take any message for him?
Mr Ashutosh	:	Yes. Please tell him that Mr Ashutosh called up and asked for an urgent delivery of hundred books order to be made by tomorrow positively. The payment would be made to him at the time of delivery in cash.
Mr Gupta	:	Sure sir, I would deliver the message at the earliest.
Mr Ashutosh	:	Thank you.

[Chapter 3]

Article Writing

Sample Article

☑ *Write an article to be published in your school magazine on the topic 'Junk Food'.*

Junk Food

By Abhinav

Junk food is also known as fast food. We prefer to eat junk food as it is easily available, affordable and tasty. ← (2) Introduction/ Starting

Most of us don't know that it is hazardous to our health. Eating junk food on a regular basis causes lack of concentration, heart disease and other ailments. Junk food contains zero or very less nutritive value. So, consuming junk food is harmful as it also leads to fat accumulation in our body thereby causing obesity. Research has also shown that children who eat junk food are inactive and are prone to stress and anxiety. ← (3) Content of the Article

We as students must reduce our intake of junk food as much as we can and cultivate the habit of eating home-cooked food. ← (4) Ending of the Article

(1) Suitable title/heading → Junk Food

Points to be kept in mind while writing an Article

- An article should have an interesting and catchy title.
- It should carry the name of the writer.
- An article is divided into a suitable number of paragraphs with an introduction, body and ending/conclusion. The division generally depends upon the word limit and the theme of the article.
- Ideas to be covered in the article should be well thought of, written in an organised and coherent style.

PRACTICE Questions

1 Write an article to be published in the school magazine entitled 'Discipline : A Key to Success' in 150 words.

2 Based on the visual clues write an article on 'Hard Work : A Key to Success' in 150 words.

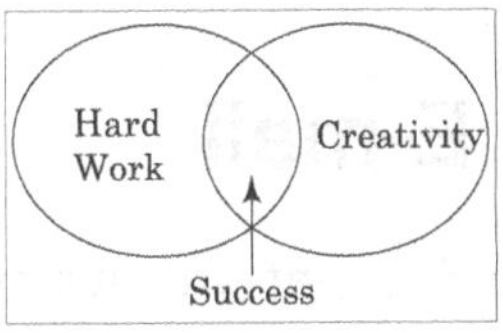

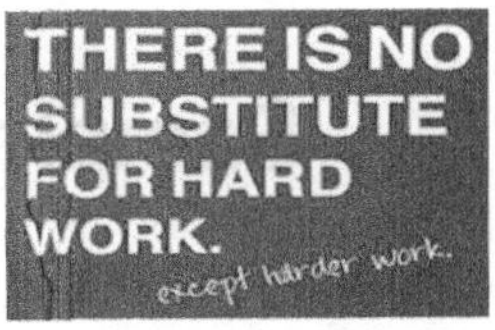

3 You are Rahul/Radhika. Write an article to be published in the newspaper in the weekly column.

- Titled 'Road Rage : A Dangerous Killer'.
- Road Rage : Kills many people.
- Reason : Impatience and lack of concern for others.
- Awareness needed.
- People should be educated and sensitised.
- Strict punishment for offenders.

4 Based on the visual clue write an article on 'Global Peace: Need of the Hour'.

5 Being a reporter you are asked to address audience on the topic 'Role of Media'. Write the same highlighting its pros and cons in an article.

6 Write an article on 'Literacy : A Boon' based on the given verbal inputs.

- Literacy : Important at all levels.
- Education is needed for growth and development.
- Individual literacy equals to country's progress.
- Efforts to be made by parents, teachers, society and government.

[Chapter 4]

E-mail Writing

Sample E-mail

☑ *Write an e-mail to your friend who lives in a different city inviting him to spend his vacation at your place.*

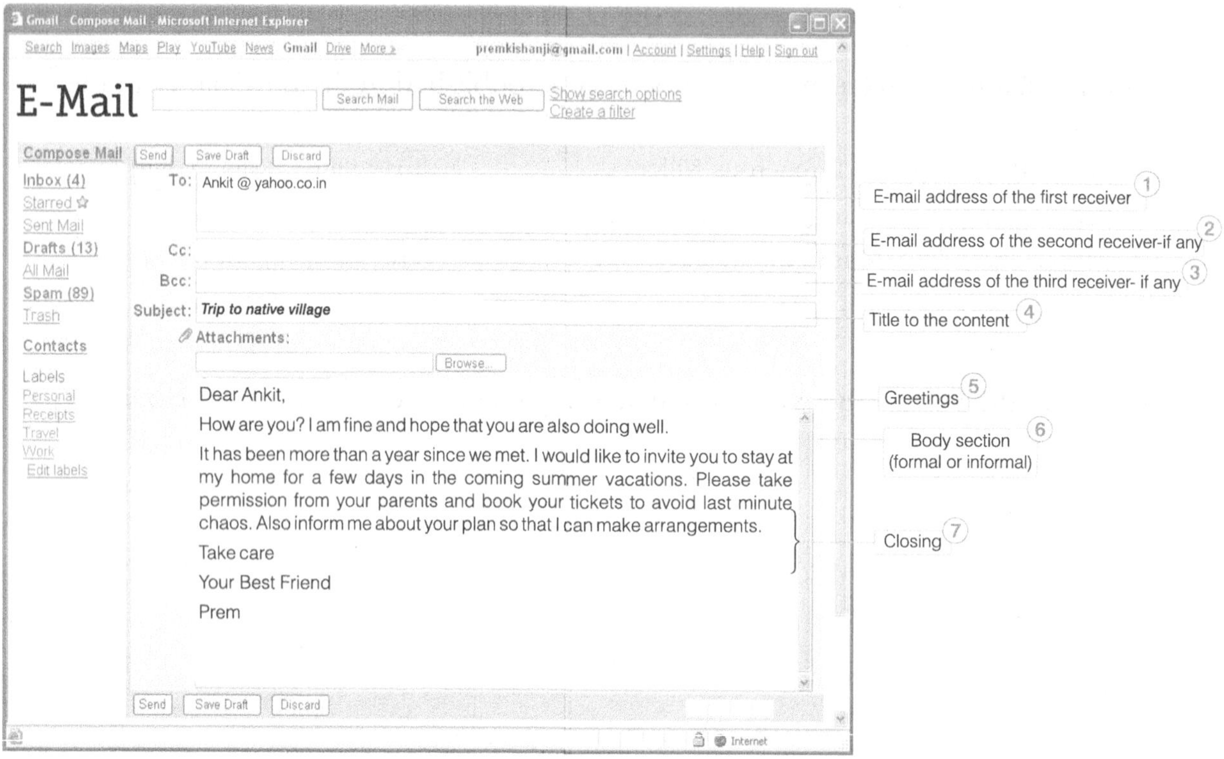

Points to be kept in mind while writing an E-mail

- At the top, receiver's address should be properly and clearly written. Subject should be short and to the point.
- It may be a formal e-mail or an informal e-mail. So greeting and salutation should be suitably written.
- The body (main content) may have two/three paragraphs i.e. different paragraph for different idea.
- Avoid SMS language.
- In conclusion space write complimentary phrase according to the relation with the person you are writing to 'Yours sincerely'- when you know the person, 'Yours faithfully'- when you have addressed it as Dear Sir/Madam).

PRACTICE Questions

1 As Akash Gupta of Billabong School, write an e-mail to the Director of National Science Museum requesting him to give permission for a visit to the museum by the students of your school on the upcoming 'Science Day'.

2 Write an e-mail to your friend telling him/her about your recent family trip to Maldives. Mention the details like places you visited, food, scenic beauty etc.

3 Write an e-mail to your favourite teacher on the occasion of 'Teachers' Day'. You can describe your feelings for your teacher with the help of the given visuals.

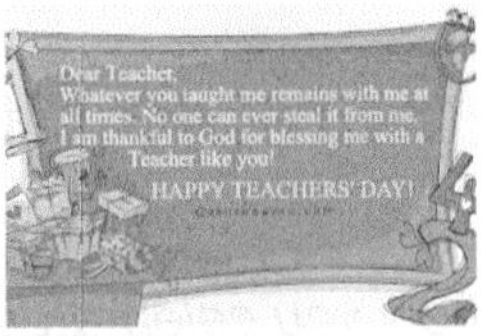

4 Your brother is away from home, studying in an engineering college. Write an e-mail to him on his twentieth birthday.

5 Based on the following visual write an e-mail to the President of your colony highlighting the problem of garbage and littering in the colony and the various diseases caused by this. Express your views while highlighting the importance of cleanliness and the need for maintaining it.

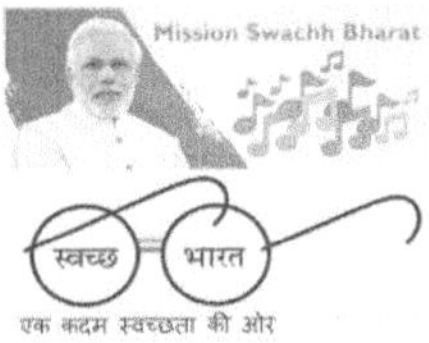

6 Your school bus stop is quite far away from your house. It becomes difficult for you to reach the bus stop due to which you miss your bus. Write an e-mail to the Principal of your school requesting her to change your bus stop.

7 Write an e-mail to Daily Publishers mentioning about your order of latest Harry Potter book. Also request them to send the order within four days as you have to gift the book to a friend on his birthday.

[Chapter 5]

Diary Entry

Sample Diary Writing

☑ *Write a diary entry on how you celebrated your birthday.*

Date → 25th September

Dear Diary,

I have turned 12 today. My parents were the first one to wish me happy birthday. I went to school. It was a usual day at school, but I was very excited. I gave my friends a small party in the lunch time. They wished me and thanked me for the party. My parents had organised a party at my home too. Friends from my neighbourhood came to the party. I cut the cake and distributed among them. They gave me gifts and thanked me for the wonderful treat. When the party was over, I opened the gifts. ← Content of the Diary Entry

Writer's name → Amit

Points to be kept in mind while writing a Diary Entry

- It is written in informal and creative language, but still follows a specific format.
- Address the diary as 'Dear Diary', if you like.
- Language should be emotionally charged since the writer writes exactly what he/she feels.
- An entry should not exceed 150 words.

PRACTICE Questions

1 You recently participated in a 'Blood Donation Camp' along with your friends. Write about the experience of doing so in a diary entry.

2 You are Shikha/Shikhar. You visited the modern art exhibition where you saw wonderful paintings and photographs by great artists from all over the world. Write a diary entry describing your visit.

3 You went to 'Delhi Automobiles Fair' with your family. Write a diary entry about your experience of the fair and what you liked the most in the fair.

4 Independence day was celebrated with great fervour and enthusiasm in your locality. Write a diary entry about how it was celebrated and what you have learnt from this glorious day.

5 You visited your sister staying in London. Write a diary entry describing your visit to abroad and what cultural differences you found between the two countries i.e. United Kingdom and India.

Chapter 6

Letter Writing

Sample Letter (Formal)

☑ *Write a letter to your Principal for granting you leave for 2 days on the occasion of your sister's wedding.*

(1) Receiver Name/rank and address →
The Principal
Happy School
Daryaganj
New Delhi-110003

(2) Date → 26th September, 20XX

(3) Subject → **Subject** Leave for 2 days on occasion of sister's wedding

(4) Salutation → Sir/Ma'am

(5) Content of the letter → I am a student of Class 7th B of your school. I would be unable to attend school on 29th and 30th September, 20XX (Tuesday and Wednesday) due to my sister's wedding.

Kindly grant me leave for 2 days.

Thanking you

(6) Subscription → Yours obediently

(7) Name and Signature →
Karan Nagpal
Roll No. 27

The letter given above is an application to school authorities. We write formal letters for many other reasons to many other people including editors, Managers or Heads of offices, government officials. In these formal letters, sender's address is added before Receiver's address and the Date is placed between the sender's and the receiver's address.

PRACTICE Questions

1 You are Aradhya Verma, 7-C, Oakland Public School. Write a letter to the Principal asking her to issue a migration certificate to you as you have to change your school due to your father's transfer to another city.

2 You are Arpit Sharma of Neel Public School.Your father is a lower clerk in a Government Institution and is unable to meet the expenses of your school education. Write an application to the Principal of your school requesting her to grant you full fee concession mentioning your good academic and sports record till now in the school.

3 As the Head Boy of your school, write a letter to the Principal requesting him/her to organise an excursion to Rishikesh for an adventure holiday like white water rafting, rock climbing and mountaineering.

4 Write a letter to the Sports Incharge of your school suggesting him to introduce Yoga in the sports curriculum of all the classes.

5 Write a letter to the librarian of your school requesting her to issue a duplicate library card to you as you have lost your original card few days ago in the school.

6 Write a letter to the Editor of 'National Times' expressing your concern over the stray dog menace in your housing society. You can use the given clues.

- Residents terrified of dog attacks.
- Can't go outside.
- Dogs attack children in the park, at roads.
- Enter houses and damage things.
- Should be caught and sterilised.

7 Write a letter to the Manager of Gaming Company Ltd requesting him to send you the catalogue (list) of the latest video games.

8 Write a letter to the Head of Local Area Network Provider complaining about the poor wi-fi connection in your area. Also mention the poor maintenance of the wires leading to the loss of network.

9 Write a letter to the SHO of your area complaining about the recent robberies and deteriorating law and order situation in your housing society. Also suggest measures to combat this problem.

10 You are Rishi Arora a resident of Delhi. Write a letter to Shoppingzone.com complaining that you have so far not received the school bag which you ordered online on their website. Invent all necessary details.

Sample Letter (Informal)

Write a letter to your uncle inviting him to your birthday party.

(1) Sender's Address →	A-59, Kailash Colony New Delhi
(2) Date →	25th September, 20XX
(3) Salutation →	Dear Uncle
	How are you? We are fine and hope that you are also doing well.
(4) Main content of the letter →	As you know that my birthday is on 5th October, so my parents are hosting a small party at our home on this occasion. I would like you to be a part of this party. Please come one day in advance and confirm your train timings so that we can come to pick you at the station.
(5) Subscription →	With lots of love
(6) First name or signature →	Sankalp

PRACTICE Questions

1 Write a letter of condolence to your friend who recently lost his father in a car accident.

2 You are Richa. Write a letter inviting your cousin, Rachna, to spend her winter break in your city i.e. Delhi. You can prepare the sightseeing plan and mention other recreational activities that you intend to do in the letter.

3 Write a letter to your younger brother living in a hostel about the benefits of early rising. You should also urge him to become an early riser for proper growth and progress.

4 Write a letter to your mother telling her about your new school. Include details like nature of teachers, mode of studies, friends etc.

5 Write a letter to your younger sister telling her about the need for honesty and patriotism in today's corrupt times. Make your letter inspiring and motivating for her to become a responsible and honest citizen.

Chapter 7

Story Writing

Sample Story

☑ *Write a story based on the given clues.*

A woman going to town—carrying a pail of milk—sell the milk in the town—starts dreaming will buy some hens from the money earned by selling milk—the hens will lay eggs everyday—will sell eggs and earn more money—purchase new dress—if anyone asks her the secret of earning so much money—she will nod her head—and she nodded her head—the pail of milk fell down

A Greedy Woman ← Title (1)

A woman was going to town and was carrying a pail of milk on her head. She wanted to sell the milk and earn money. She started day-dreaming. She thought that she would buy some hens from the money she will get by selling milk. The hens will lay eggs every morning. She would sell those eggs and become rich. She planned to purchase new dresses. When people will ask her as to how she became rich, she would nod her head. And she nodded her head in reality. The pail of milk fell down and the milk spilled all over the ground. ← Content (2)

Points to be kept in mind while writing a Story

- A story should have a title.
- The narrative should have a single incident.
- Language should be interesting and effective.
- It should be written in the past tense.
- As a form of creative art, it should be original.
- Beginning of the story should capture the reader's attention.
- All events should be interconnected.
- There should be a main character in the story.
- The entire narrative should be planned before starting to write.
- A story should have a message for the readers.
- The ending should leave a lasting effect on the readers.

Type I : Based on Verbal Inputs

1 Write a beautiful story with the help of the given verbal clues entitled 'Struggles make us shine'.

A man had passion of watching butterflies—once found a butterfly coming out of cocoon—it was trying very hard—man sat there waiting for it—it couldn't come out after several hours—man decided to help—cut the cocoon a bit—butterfly came out—with a swollen body and withered wings—man thought it would fly after sometime—it couldn't—it came out without struggling—as a result the fluid inside it was not released so the body swelled—the butterfly couldn't fly!—Moral: struggles are necessary—make us better and mature

2 With the help of the given verbal clues, write a story in your own words with a suitable title and moral.

Mahatma Gandhi was on country expedition—was urging people to donate funds for freedom struggle—went to Odisha—addressed a crowd there—after the speech a poor old woman with torn clothes got up—tried to reach him, but was shoved away—finally reached him and placed a copper coin at his feet—went away quietly—he took the coin and kept it safely—his accomplice asked the reason —Gandhiji replied—this coin is too precious—given by a poor, old woman who has nothing—in service of the country

Type II : Based on Visual Inputs

1 Write a story in your own words keeping in mind the given visual clue. You can make it as interesting and creative as possible alongwith a title and a relevant moral.

2 Write a short story with the help of the given visual clue. Also provide your story with a suitable title and a moral.

3 Write a story with the help of the given visual clue. Give your story a title and a relevant moral.

Type III : Based on Verbal and Visual Inputs

1 Draw a beautiful story based on the given verbal and visual clues.

Two close friends lived together—fought many times—never gave up friendship—went on a voyage—got stuck in the desert storm—had food and water with them—one of them wanted to complete the little water they had—other suggested we should drink little by little—that way it would last longer—fought on the issue—the mature one slapped the other—one wrote on the sand 'my friend slapped me'—moved again—found an oasis after few days—were very happy—the friend who was slapped started bathing in the spring—was about to drown—his friend saves him—again he writes 'my friend saved me' on stone—friend asks why he wrote on sand and stone—he says 'bad things written on sand'—will be removed soon—good things written on stone—will always be there.

2 On the basis of the given verbal and visual clues construct a story in your words.Your story should carry a moral and an apt title.

Father and son travelling by train—a group of noisy youngsters also travelling—son observes everything—seems to be over excited—shouts and screams while seeing things outside the train—friends make fun of the boy—call him mad for being over excited—father replies patiently—son born blind—was operated recently—is seeing ordinary things for the first time—that's why excited—friends feel ashamed and say sorry to the duo.

Reading

Worksheet 1

Directions *Read the following passages carefully and answer the questions that follow.*

1 Raksha Bandhan is a Hindu festival that celebrates love and bond between brothers and sisters. It falls on the full moon day (Shravan Poornima) of the Shravan month of the Hindu lunisolar Nepali calendar. Therefore, it is also called Rakhi Purnima in many parts of India and is observed by Hindus and Jains. It is celebrated in India, Mauritius and Nepal.

It is an ancient festival, dating back 6000 years to the Indus Valley Civilisation. It has many myths and historic legends linked to it e.g. the Rajput queens practiced the custom of sending rakhis to neighbouring rulers as token of love and brotherhood. On Raksha Bandhan, sisters tie a 'rakhi' (sacred thread) on her brother's wrist.

This symbolises the sister's love and prayers for her brother's well-being and the brother's life-long vow to protect her.

(i) Why is Raksha Bandhan known as 'Rakhi Purnima'?

(ii) What custom was followed by the Rajput queens?

(iii) What does Raksha Bandhan symbolises?

(iv) The synonym of 'vow' is

(v) The antonym of 'tie' is

2 Sarvepalli Radhakrishnan was born on 5th September, 1888 in a Telugu family in Thiruttani village near the border of Andhra Pradesh and Tamil Nadu. His father was a revenue official in the service of a local landlord. As his father was poor, Radhakrishnan supported most of his education through scholarships. Radhakrishnan was a philosopher and statesman. He was the first Vice-President and the second President of India. He was awarded with several awards during his life, including a knighthood in 1931.

He was also awarded the highest civilian award in India, Bharat Ratna in 1954 and honorary membership of the British Royal Order of Merit in 1963. Radhakrishnan believed that "teachers should be the best minds in the country". Since 1962, his birthday is celebrated as Teachers' Day. He died on 17 April 1975, at the age of 86.

(i) Who was Sarvepalli Radhakrishnan?

(ii) What was his view about teachers?

(iii) Where is Thiruttani village situated in India?

(iv) Find a proper noun from the passage.

(v) Find a word from the passage that means 'a skilled, experienced and respected political leader or figure'.

Worksheet 2

Directions *Read the following passages carefully and answer the questions that follow.*

1 Raghu was a famous sculptor. His sculptures looked real. One day he saw a dream that after fifteen days, the demon of death would take him. He prepared nine statues of himself. On the 15th day, he heard him coming. He took his place between the statues. The Demon could not recognise him. He was astonished to see ten Raghus. He returned to the God of death and told everything. The God decided to visit Raghu himself. Raghu stood motionless. The God initially got perplexed. The God said: "Raghu, these sculptures would have been perfect, but for one mistake." Raghu was unable to suffer the least blemish in his work. He came out and asked, "Where is the fault?" The God caught him and said, "Here". The statues were faultless but Raghu was caught because of his pride.

(i) What did Raghu see in his dream?

(ii) Why did Raghu prepare nine statues?

(iii) Why did the God of death decide to visit Raghu?

(iv) Find an adverb from the line " The God initially got perplexed."

(v) Find a word in the passage that means 'an evil spirit or devil.'

2 The elephant is the largest four-legged animal in the world. It is found in the forests of Asia and Africa. Though not the tallest animal in the world, its huge size and weight makes it the largest animal. A fully grown elephant is ten or eleven feet high. It has four strong pillar like legs. It has a large head and a short neck. Its eyes are small. It has a pair of ears like big fans.

The most important part of the body is its trunk which is a long nose which reaches to the ground. It also serves as a hand for holding things like coconut leaves and as an arm for lifting weights. The elephant can lift its trunk filled with water and then blow it into its mouth or over its body. Adult elephants have tusks as front teeth. As the back teeth of the elephant get worn away, new ones appear. Elephants may look slow in moving, but they can walk fast as well as long distances. They are good swimmers too. They can be tamed and trained. In olden days they were used in warfare. Today, they are used to pull down huge trees and to carry huge logs.

(i) Where are elephants generally found?

(ii) Mention any two characteristics of fully grown elephant.

(iii) How is the trunk useful in drinking water?

(iv) Write the antonym of 'found'.

(v) Write the synonym of 'important'.

Worksheet 3

Directions *Read the following passages carefully and answer the questions that follow.*

1 Former Indian cricketer, Sachin Tendulkar was born on 24th April, 1973. He is regarded as one of the greatest cricketers of all time. He started playing cricket at the age of eleven and made his Test debut on 15th November, 1989 against Pakistan at the age of 16. He is the only player to have scored one hundred international centuries and the first batsman to score a double century in a One Day International. He holds the record for most number of runs in both ODI and Test cricket. He is the only player to complete over 30000 runs in international cricket.

Tendulkar was a part of the Indian team that won the 2011 World Cup. He received Arjuna Award in 1994 for his outstanding achievement in cricket, the Rajiv Gandhi Khel Ratna Award in 1997, the Padma Shri and Padma Vibhushan Awards in 1999 and 2008, respectively. He is the youngest recipient and the first ever sportsperson to receive Bharat Ratna, India's highest civilian award.

He also won the 2010 Sir Garfield Sobers Trophy for cricketer of the year at the ICC Awards. In 2012, Tendulkar was nominated to the Rajya Sabha. In December 2012, he announced his retirement from ODIs. He retired from Twenty-20 cricket in October, 2013 and subsequently announced his retirement from all forms of cricket in November, 2013.

(i) List all the awards won by Sachin Tendulkar.

____

(ii) When did Tendulkar announce his retirement from ODIs and Twenty-20?

____

(iii) Why is Sachin Tendulkar regarded as one of the greatest cricketers of all time?

____

(iv) Find a word from the passage that means 'formally enter as a candidate.'

____

(v) A person who plays cricket is called _______________

2 Emperor Akbar was habitual of putting riddles and puzzles to his courtiers. He often asked questions which were strange and witty. It took much wisdom to answer these questions. Once he asked a very strange question. The courtiers were astonished by his question. Akbar glanced at his courtiers to seek answers. As he looked at each one of them, their heads began to hang low in search of an answer. It was at this moment that Birbal entered the courtyard.

Birbal was well aware of the emperor's nature and quickly grasped the situation and asked: "May I know the question so that I can try for an answer." Akbar said: "How many crows are there in this city?" Without even a moment's thought, Birbal replied: "There are fifty thousand five hundred and eighty nine crows, my lord." "How can you be so sure about this number?" Asked the emperor.

Birbal said: "Make your men count them, my lord. If you find more crows it means some have come to visit their relatives in the city. If you find less number of crows, it means some have gone to visit their relatives outside the city." Akbar was well pleased by Birbal's wit. He announced rewards for Birbal.

(i) What kind of questions did Emperor Akbar ask?

____

(ii) Do you think Birbal was intelligent? Give a reason to support your answer.

____

(iii) What was Birbal's response to Akbar?

____

(iv) Find an adjective from the line "Once he asked a very strange question."

____

(v) Write the antonym of 'reward'.

____

Worksheet 4

Directions *Read the following passages carefully and answer the questions that follow.*

1 The Himalayas, meaning 'abode of snow', is a mountain range in South Asia which separates the Indo-Gangetic plain from Tibetan plateau. This range is home to nine of the ten highest peaks on Earth, including the highest above sea level, Mount Everest. The Himalayas are bordered on the North by the Tibetan plateau, on the South by the Indo-Gangetic plain, on the North-West by the Karakoram and Hindu Kush ranges and on the East by Assam and Arunachal Pradesh.

The Himalayas runs through five countries - India, Nepal, Bhutan, Tibet and Pakistan, with the first three countries having sovereignty over most of the range. The Himalayan range runs North-West to South-East in a 2400 km long arc. The range varies in width from 400 km in the West to 150 km in the East. Besides the Greater Himalayas, there are several parallel lower ranges. The southernmost of these are called the Shivalik hills. Further North is a higher range, reaching two to three thousand meters, known as the lower Himalayan range.

Three of the world's major rivers - the Indus, the Ganges and the Brahmaputra originate in the Himalayas. While the Indus and the Brahmaputra rise near Mount Kailash in Tibet, the Ganges rises in Uttarakhand. Their combined drainage basin is home to some 600 million people.

(i) What do you mean by the word 'Himalayas'?

(ii) What are Shivalik hills?

(iii) Name the rivers that originate in the Himalayas.

(iv) Write the superlative degree of the word 'high'.

(v) What is the synonym of 'sovereignty'?

2 Once, there was a cap-seller in a town. He was a very hard working man. On one fine day, he was selling caps from one place to another. "Caps, caps, caps....Five rupees, ten rupees....come and buy caps." After selling few caps, he felt very tired because of moving here and there. He decided to sit for few minutes, under a big tree, and take rest.

Soon, he slept off. He was unaware that there were monkeys all around. The monkeys, sitting on the big tree, saw the cap-seller sleeping. The monkeys were sitting on the top of the tree. They came down, took the caps from the cap-seller's bag and wore them.

They again climbed on the top of the tree. When the cap-seller woke up, he could not find his caps. He was shocked to see his basket empty. He searched for his caps everywhere. To his surprise, he saw the monkeys were wearing them.

He found that the monkeys were imitating him. So, he understood how he will get back those caps. He started throwing his cap. The monkeys started imitating him and threw their caps down. The cap-seller collected all the caps, put them back in his basket and went away happily.

(i) Why did the cap-seller decide to take rest under a tree?

....

(ii) What happened when the cap-seller woke up?

....

(iii) How did the cap-seller manage to get his caps back?

....

(iv) Write the antonym of 'aware'.

....

(v) Find a word from the passage that means 'copy a person's mannerism especially for comic effect.'

....

Worksheet 5

Directions *Read the following passages carefully and answer the questions that follow.*

1 A milkman became very wealthy through dishonest means. He had to cross a river every day to reach a city where his customers lived. He mixed the water of the river with the milk that he sold for a good profit. One day, he went around collecting the dues in order to celebrate the wedding of his son. With the large amount thus, collected, he purchased plenty of expensive clothes and glittering gold ornaments.

But while crossing the river the boat capsized and all his costly purchases were swallowed by the river. The milk vendor was speechless with grief. At that time he heard a voice that came from the river, "Do not weep. What you have lost is only the illicit gains you earned through cheating your customers."

(i) What did the milkman do with the milk?

(a) He mixed hay with the milk ☐ (b) He did nothing ☐

(c) He mixed water with the milk ☐ (d) All of these ☐

(ii) Who swallowed the expensive clothes and gold ornaments?

(a) Milk ☐ (b) River ☐

(c) Boat ☐ (d) None of these ☐

(iii) What did the milkman hear?

(a) He heard a voice coming from the river ☐

(b) He heard songs ☐

(c) He heard music ☐

(d) He heard the sound made by the river ☐

(iv) Make adjective from the word 'profit.'

(a) Perfect ☐ (b) Profitly ☐

(c) Profitable ☐ (d) Profits ☐

(v) Make noun from the word 'celebrate.'

(a) Celebrated ☐ (b) Celebrating ☐

(c) Collect ☐ (d) Celebration ☐

2 An earthquake is the noticeable shaking of the earth's surface, which can be violent enough to destroy major buildings and kill thousands of people. Earthquakes have destroyed many cities. They result from the sudden release of energy in the Earth's crust that creates seismic waves. An earthquake's point of origin is called its focus or hypocenter. The epicenter is the point at ground level directly above the hypocenter. Often the main earthquake is preceded by number of foreshocks and followed by aftershocks.

Earthquakes are measured using observations from seismometers. They can also be measured on the local magnitude scale, referred to as the Richter scale. Magnitude 3 or lower earthquakes are almost imperceptible or weak and magnitude 7 or over cause serious damages. The earthquake of 9.0 magnitude hit Japan in 2011 and was the largest intensity earthquake since records began. Earthquakes can also trigger landslides and volcanic activity.

(i) What is an earthquake?

(a) It is a landslide ☐

(b) It is a noticeable shaking of the earth's surface ☐

(c) It is a flood caused by rivers ☐

(d) All of the above ☐

(ii) Why does an earthquake occur?

(a) It occurs due to volcanic eruptions ☐

(b) It occurs due to global warming ☐

(c) It occurs due to release of energy from the Earth's crust ☐

(d) It occurs to destroy buildings ☐

(iii) How do we measure an earthquake?

(a) Through seismometers ☐

(b) Through a weighing machine ☐

(c) Through a calculator ☐

(d) All of the above ☐

(iv) Write the comparative degree of the word 'large.'

(a) Largest ☐ (b) More large ☐

(c) Most large ☐ (d) Larger ☐

(v) Make adverb from the word 'sudden'.

(a) Suddenly ☐ (b) Sorrow ☐

(c) Suddened ☐ (d) Suddening ☐

Worksheet 6

Directions *Read the following passages carefully and answer the questions that follow.*

1 Yoga is a physical, mental and spiritual discipline that originated in India. 21st June is now being celebrated as International Yoga Day, declared by United Nations General Assembly (UNGA) on 11th December, 2014. Indian Prime Minister Narendra Modi, in his UN address, suggested that 21st June should be adopted as Yoga Day. It is the longest day of the year (Summer Solstice) in the Northern Hemisphere and has special significance in many parts of the world. From the point of view of Yoga, the Summer Solstice marks the transition to Dakshinayana.

The first full Moon after Summer Solstice is known as Guru Poornima. Lord Shiva, the first Yoga practitioner, is said to have started imparting the knowledge of yoga to rest of the mankind on this day. Dakshinayana is also considered a good time to pursue spiritual practices. The declaration of this day came after the call for the adoption by PM Modi during his address at UNGA on 27th September, 2014. The first Yoga Day was observed worldwide on 21st June, 2015. More than 35000 people, including PM Modi and a large number of dignitaries from 84 nations, performed Yoga for 35 minutes at Rajpath in New Delhi. The day devoted to Yoga was observed by millions across the world.

(i) When do we celebrate International Yoga Day?

(a) 27th September, 2014 ☐ (b) 21st June ☐

(c) 11th December, 2014 ☐ (d) All of these ☐

(ii) Who declared 21st June to be the International Yoga Day?

(a) Prime Minister Narendra Modi ☐ (b) United Nations General Assembly ☐

(c) Lord Shiva ☐ (d) All of these ☐

(iii) What is Summer Solstice?

(a) The first full Moon day after 21st June ☐

(b) The first full Moon day before 21st June ☐

(c) The longest day of the year in the Northern Hemisphere ☐

(d) None of the above ☐

(iv) Make noun from the word 'adopt'.

(a) Adopted ☐ (b) Adobe ☐

(c) Adept ☐ (d) Adoption ☐

(v) Give one word for - a person actively engaged in an art, discipline or profession.

(a) Practitioner ☐ (b) Practice ☐

(c) Practicing ☐ (d) Skill ☐

2 Once, there was a wise king. He had two sons. He appointed eminent scholars to teach them all subjects. After a few years of teachings, the king badly fell ill. So, he wanted to select his next heir for his kingdom. He wanted to test his sons' abilities. He called both of them and gave a room to each of them. He said: "You must fill this room completely with anything you wish. It can be anything! But there should be no space left behind and you should not seek any advice from anyone."

The next day the king visited his elder son's room. The room was filled with hay. The king sighed on the foolishness of the elder son. Then he went to his younger son's room. But it was kept closed. The king knocked at the door of the room.

The younger son asked his father to come inside and close the door. There was darkness everywhere. The king shouted at his younger son. The younger son lighted a candle and said: "I have filled this room with light!" The king felt very happy and proudly hugged his son. He understood that the younger son would be the right person to rule the kingdom after him.

(i) What did the king want to do?

(a) He wanted to sleep for long hours ☐

(b) He wanted to visit a doctor ☐

(c) He wanted to test his sons' abilities ☐

(d) He wanted eminent scholars ☐

(ii) The elder son filled his room with

(a) people ☐ (b) hay ☐

(c) vegetables ☐ (d) fruits ☐

(iii) Who filled his room with light?

(a) Elder son ☐ (b) King ☐

(c) Scholar ☐ (d) Younger son ☐

(iv) Make adjective from the word 'proudly'.

(a) Proud ☐ (b) Arrogance ☐

(c) Pride ☐ (d) None of these ☐

(v) Give another word for 'advice'.

(a) Complete ☐ (b) Close ☐

(c) Suggestion ☐ (d) Seek ☐

Worksheet 7

Directions *Read the following poems carefully and answer the questions that follow.*

1

Why do you sit there on the floor so quiet and silent, tell me, mother dear?
The rain is coming in through the open window, making you all wet and you don't mind it.
Do you hear the gong striking four? It is time for my brother to come home from school.
What has happened to you that you look so strange?
Haven't you got a letter from father today?
I saw the postman bringing letters in his bag for almost everybody in the town.
Only father's letters he keeps to read himself. I am sure the postman is a wicked man.
But don't be unhappy about that, mother dear.
Tomorrow is market day in the next village. You ask your maid to buy some pens and papers.
I myself will write all father's letters.

(i) What has the mother been waiting for?

____

(ii) Why does the poet call the postman wicked?

____

(iii) What does he suggest to make the mother happy?

____

(iv) From the poem, find the antonym of the word 'happy.'

____

(v) From the poem find the homophone of 'made.'

____

2

What are you busy with. O vibrant bee?
I am busy collecting honey with glee!
What do you do with the collected honey…O beautiful bee?
I preserve it in my home, sweet home… come and see!
What do you do in your home, sweet home… O my busy bee?
I enjoy the taste of honey….. want to join me !
What will you do if I destroy your home… my lovely bee?
Then very violent will my nature turn to be!
I will sting and sting and chase thee.

(i) What does the bee do all day long?

(ii) Where does the bee keep all the honey?

(iii) When does the bee's nature become violent?

(iv) Explain the meaning of the word 'preserve.'

(v) Write two words that rhyme with.

(a) Bee

(b) Chase

(c) Sting

Worksheet 8

Directions *Read the following poems carefully and answer the questions that follow.*

1

'When I wast at the party',
Said Betty, aged just four,
'A little girl fell off her chair
Right down upon the floor,
And all the other little girls
Began to laugh, but me—
I didn't laugh a single bit,'
Said Betty seriously.
'Why not?'— her mother asked her,
Full of delight to find
That Betty— bless her little heart!
Had been so sweetly kind.
'Why didn't you laugh, my darling?
Or don't you like to tell?'
'I didn't laugh,' said Betty,
'Because it was I that fell.'

(i) How old was Betty?

(a) Three years ☐ (b) Four years ☐

(c) Six years ☐ (d) None of these ☐

(ii) Why did the little girls laugh?

(a) A little girl broke her chair ☐

(b) They were full of delight ☐

(c) A little girl fell off her chair ☐

(d) They decided to sit on the floor ☐

(iii) Betty didn't laugh because

(a) her best friend fell off her chair ☐

(b) she was the one who fell off her chair ☐

(c) she was sympathetic towards her best friend ☐

(d) her mother had taught her not to laugh ☐

(iv) From the poem find the synonym of the word 'generous'.

(a) Delight ☐ (b) Single ☐ (c) Bless ☐ (d) Kind ☐

(v) From the poem find the antonym of the word 'casually.'

(a) Laughing ☐ (b) Seriously ☐ (c) Sweetly ☐ (d) Little ☐

2

The tool unused lies lost in dust,
The sword unused turns dull with rust,
The path unused grows clogged with weed,
The crop untended goes to seed.
Skills unused will soon decay,
Talents wasted, fade away.
I will work with a wish and I'll work with a will,
And the task that life brings me I'll gladly fulfill,
And unfolding new skills, many joys shall be mine.
Away dull rust! Let me shine!

(i) What will happen if you do not use your skills?

(a) It will encourage you to do good things ☐

(b) It will soon decay or die ☐

(c) It will make you shine ☐

(d) It will make you happy ☐

(ii) How should a person work to get positive results?

(a) He should work without a wish ☐

(b) He should work without a will ☐

(c) He should work with both will and wish ☐

(d) All of the above ☐

(iii) What will happen to unused sword?

(a) It will turn dull with rust ☐ (b) It will shine ☐

(c) Nothing will happen to it ☐ (d) It will break ☐

(iv) Give one word for - a wild plant growing where it is not wanted and in competition with cultivated plants.

(a) Deed ☐ (b) Seed ☐ (c) Need ☐ (d) Weed ☐

(v) Write a word that rhymes with 'decay' in the above poem.

(a) Stay ☐ (b) Fade ☐ (c) Away ☐ (d) Will ☐

Answers

Prose

1. Three Questions

Extract Based Questions

1. (iv) (c) (v) (a) 2. (iv) (c) (v) (a)

True or False

1. True 2. False 3. True 4. False

2. A Gift of Chappals

Extract Based Questions

1. (iv) (c) (v) (a) 2. (iv) (d) (v) (c)

True or False

1. True 2. False 3. False 4. False 5. False

3. Gopal and the Hilsa-Fish

Extract Based Questions

1. (iv) (c) (v) (d) 2. (iv) (b) (v) (a)

True or False

1. False 2. False 3. True 4. True 5. True

4. The Ashes that Made Trees Bloom

Extract Based Questions

1. (iv) (b) (v) (c) 2. (iv) (d) (v) (a)

True or False

1. False 2. True 3. False 4. True 5. False

Fill in the Blanks

1. followed 2. chopped off 3. arriving
4. went

5. Quality

Extract Based Questions

1. (iv) (a) (v) (d) 2. (iv) (d) (v) (b)

True or False

1. True 2. False 3. False 4. True 5. False

6. Expert Detectives

Extract Based Questions

1. (iv) (c) (v) (d) 2. (iv) (b) (v) (a)

True or False

1. False 2. False 3. True 4. True 5. False

Fill in the Blanks

1. doubtful 2. immediately 3.quietly
4. discussion 5. investigation

7. The Invention of Vita-Wonk

Extract Based Questions

1. (iv) (c) (v) (d) 2. (iv) (d) (v) (b)

True or False

1. False 2. True 3. False 4. False
5. True

Poetry

1. The Squirrel

Extract Based Questions

1. (iv) (a) (v) (d) 2. (iv) (c) (v) (b)

2. The Rebel

Extract Based Questions

1. (iv) (b) (v) (d) 2. (iv) (a) (v) (c)

Fill in the Blanks

1. long 2. safe 3. severely
4. suddenly

3. The Shed

Extract Based Questions

1. (iv) (b) (v) (a)
2. (iv) (c) (v) (d)

4. Chivvy

Extract Based Questions

1. (iv) (b) (v) (d) 2. (iv) (a) (v) (d)

Fill in the Blanks

1. dragging 2. shut 3. make 4. take
5. interrupted

5. Trees

Extract Based Questions

1. (iv) (c) (v) (a) 2. (iv) (b) (v) (c)

6. Mystery of the Talking Fan

Extract Based Questions

1. (iv) (c) (v) (d) 2. (iv) (a) (v) (c)

7. Dad and the Cat and the Tree

Extract Based Questions

1. (iv) (c) (v) (a) 2. (iv) (c) (v) (b)

8. Meadow Surprises

Extract Based Questions

1. (iv) (b) (v) (c) 2. (iv) (a) (v) (d)

True or False

1. True 2. False 3. True 4. False
5. Flase

9. Garden Snake

Extract Based Questions

1. (iv) (d) (v) (a) 2. (iv) (b) (v) (c)

Supplementary

1. The Tiny Teacher

True or False

1. False 2. True 3. False 4. True 5. True

2. Bringing Up Kari

True or False

1. True 2. False 3. False 4. False 5. True

3. Golu Grows a Nose

True or False

1. True 2. False 3. False 4. True 5. True

4. Chandni

True or False

1. False 2. True 3. False 4. False 5. False

5. The Bear Story

True or False

1. False 2. False 3. True 4. True

6. A Tiger in the House

True or False

1. False 2. True 3. True 4. False 5. True

7. An Alien Hand

True or False

1. False 2. True 3. False 4. True 5. True

Grammar

1. Articles

1. (i) a (ii) a (iii) a (iv) The (v) a
2. (i) a (ii) the (iii) The (iv) A (v) an, the
3. (i) I will visit a temple in the morning.
   (ii) My father applied plans A, B and C to save the cat.
   (iii) Are you going to watch a movie today?
   (iv) I visited the shop to buy boots after two years.
   (v) What a beautiful scene!
4.

Incorrect	Correct
(i) a	the
(ii) a	an
(iii) a	the

5. (i) South Indian states are (the) major producers of coffee in India.
   (ii) Music has (an) important place in our lives.
   (iii) Life is (a) precious gift from God to us.
   (iv) China is (the) most populated country in (the) world.
   (v) (The) Koala bears are found in (the) coastal areas of Australia.
6. (i) the (ii) the (iii) a (iv) the

2. Nouns and Pronouns

1. (i) Desire (ii) Cloth (iii) Street (iv) Theatre (v) Waiter
2. (i) Starvation (ii) Disappointment (iii) Annoyance (iv) Interruption (v) Attention (vi) Discovery (vii) Wobble (viii) Goodness (ix) Dirt (x) Greatness (xi) Safety
3. (i) Mr Purcell, shop (ii) cats, dogs, shop (iii) cage (iv) shopkeeper, stool (v) rat (vi) Dehra (vii) Timothy (viii) grandfather (ix) months, home (x) leopard, cage
4. (i) (India) has a rich cultural heritage.
   (ii) (Little Red Riding Hood) immediately set out to see her sick (grandmother).
   (iii) (Coffee) is very popular in many parts of (world.)
   (iv) (Mohit) and (Preeti) went skating on (Saturday).
   (v) (Mr Nath) has written some (facts) about (Maya).
5. (i) She (ii) We, you (iii) you, his (iv) you, me (v) He
6.

Incorrect	Correct
(i) His	He
(ii) which	who
(iii) Himself	He
(iv) Him	He

7. (i) What (ii) Which (iii) Who (iv) Whose (v) Whom

3. Conjunctions

1. (i) but (ii) because (iii) or (iv) and (v) because (vi) as (vii) after (viii) When (ix) so that (x) if

2. (i) Meena gave me a cake but I didn't eat it.
(ii) I visited the Grand Canyon when I went to Arizona.
(iii) This is the place where we stayed last time we visited.
(iv) Though I came early, I couldn't get a seat.
(v) Everyone trusts her because she is honest.

3. (i) (b) (ii) (a) (iii) (d) (iv) (c) (v) (a)

4. (i) I could not catch the train, as I reached the station very late.
(ii) I respect him because he is an honest man.
(iii) He was guilty so he was punished.
(iv) I reached the clock tower, where my friend would meet me.
(v) You will not make mistakes if you pay attention to your work.

5. (i) so (ii) When (iii) as (iv) while
(v) as well as

4. Adjectives

1. (i) precious (ii) ordinary (iii) faster
(iv) famous (v) rude (vi) crowded, noisy
(vii) violent (viii) unfortunate
(ix) common (x) Pretty

2. (i) Smallest (ii) Largest (iii) Strongest
(iv) Strangest (v) Longest

3. (i) Bigger (ii) Slower (iii) Smaller
(iv) Faster (v) Harder

4. (i) Colder, Coldest (ii) Cleaner, Cleanest
(iii) Happier, Happiest (iv) Funnier, Funniest
(v) More nervous, Most nervous

5. (i) sweeter (ii) more expensive
(iii) tallest (iv) best
(v) more intelligent

6. (i) tidier (ii) more courageous
(iii) strongest (iv) last
(v) better, more intelligent
(vi) more difficult (vii) wettest
(viii) lovelier (ix) most popular
(x) stranger

7. (i) strong (ii) delicate
(iii) righteous (iv) naughty
(v) large (vi) busy
(vii) unknown (viii) ferocious
(ix) interesting (x) disturbing

5. Prepositions

1. (i) of (ii) in (iii) to (iv) of (v) of
(vi) to (vii) for (viii) of (ix) at

2. (i) Shikha loves to read.
(ii) Sharan jumped into the well.
(iii) My grandparents live in Kerala.
(iv) Romita damaged her car by hitting it against a wall.
(v) We should have a feeling of acceptability for old people.

3.

	Before	Missing	After
(i)	need	to	develop
(ii)	things	for	themselves
(iii)	need	to	acquire
(iv)	skills	of	communication

4. (i) on (ii) On, at, in, of, of
(iii) in, of (iv) of, of
(v) till, in (vi) with
(vii) about, for, to (viii) at
(ix) about (x) in, about

5.

	Incorrect	Correct
(i)	of	in
(ii)	on	of
(iii)	with	by
(iv)	about	in
(v)	in	on
(vi)	on	of

6. (i) to (ii) of (iii) with
(iv) for (v) in (vi) with
(vii) from (viii) in (ix) on
(x) with

6. Tenses

1. (i) The children will ride on his back.
(ii) He will roam freely during the day.
(iii) He will eat the same food as the dogs.
(iv) The lady will visit her sister.
(v) She will not want him to come with her.

2.

	Incorrect	Correct
(i)	are	is
(ii)	is	are
(iii)	is	are
(iv)	known	know
(v)	reading	read
(vi)	are	is
(vii)	reading	read

3. (i) She will translate the story to Hindi. (Future Tense)

(ii) Please speak in English in the class. (Present Tense)
(iii) He does not have any money to buy food. (Present Tense)
(iv) Mr Nath does not want to be friendly with Maya and Nishad. (Present Tense)
(v) They offered us a heavy discount on the new car. (Past Tense)

4. (i) scored (ii) celebrated
(iii) went, play
(iv) reached, was surprised, crouching
(v) hiding (vi) referred
(vii) went (viii) reserve
(ix) was damaged (x) filled, spurted

5. (i) Have (ii) is (iii) are
(iv) is (v) was/is (vi) am
(vii) is (viii) Is (ix) are
(x) has (xi) were/are

6. (i) write (ii) arise (iii) forgive
(iv) withdraw (v) shrink (vi) forbid

7. Verbs

1. (i) lived (ii) love (iii) do, leave
(iv) go (v) seemed

2. (i) digging (ii) serve (iii) dressed
(iv) brought (v) went

3.

Incorrect	Correct
(i) attract	attracts
(ii) produces	produce
(iii) hurt	hurts
(iv) helped	helps
(v) stick	stuck
(vi) helping	helps
(vii) keeping	keep
(viii) floss	flossing
(ix) been	be

4.

	Before	Missing	After
A. (i)	He	was	an
(ii)	He	lived	alone
(iii)	everybody	took	care
B. (i)	It	has	eight
(ii)	There	is	an
(iii)	visitor	looks	through

5. (i) Are you coming to school tomorrow?
(ii) Fantastic! We signed the deal.
(iii) He has never seen them.
(iv) The woodcutter was chopping wood in the forest.
(v) When you see these signs, you know that winter is near.

6. (i) left (ii) completed/finished, left
(iii) prepared, scored
(iv) finished/completed, left, play
(v) want/bought (vi) bought
(vii) work (viii) get
(ix) tries (x) drank

8. Adverbs

1. (i) often (ii) everyday (iii) greatly
(iv) rarely (v) so

2. (i) long (adjective) (ii) safe (adjective)
(iii) severely (adverb) (iv) suddenly (adverb)
(v) usually (adverb)

3. (i) Rapidly (ii) Promptly
(iii) Luckily (iv) Perfectly
(v) Wisely

4. (i) Adverbs — possibly, nearly, partly, suddenly
(ii) Adjectives—lively, poor, wicked, mighty, costly, foul

5. (i) Kanika was always very bad in studies.
(ii) The atmosphere is very cold at both these places.
(iii) I can recall some of my carefree moments.
(iv) The bus stopped abruptly.
(v) Soon after, the line gets disconnected.

6. (i) commonly (ii) immediately (iii) quietly
(iv) sorrowfully (v) happily (vi) ago
(vii) again (viii) already (ix) only
(x) continuously

7. (i) The plane has just taken off.
(ii) Always be prepared for the worst.
(iii) Is the drawing room big enough?
(iv) Many tradesmen, from far and wide, came to the Eid fair.
(v) Simi played the guitar skilfully.

9. Modals

1. (i) would (ii) could (iii) would
(iv) will (v) must

2. (i) Can (ii) could (iii) must
(iv) would (v) will (vi) shall
(vii) might (viii) May, may (ix) should
(x) will

3. (i) I will wait for the right opportunity to strike.
(ii) Children below the age of eighteen years must not drive.
(iii) I can also remember my frightening moments.
(iv) And what would you like to drink?
(v) We could hear the sound of music.
(vi) A small fire can be put out with a damp blanket.

4. A. **Incorrect** **Correct**
(i) should can
(ii) should could
(iii) might would

B.
(i) are is
(ii) are our
(iii) must need
(iv) an of
(v) could should
(vi) would should

5. (i) (d) (ii) (d) (iii) (b) (iv) (c)
(v) (a)

10. Determiners

1. (i) This (ii) That (iii) Those
(iv) These (v) many (vi) Some
(vii) few (viii) large (ix) first
(x) All

2. (i) this (ii) These (iii) This, that
(iv) Those (v) This

3. (i) many (ii) most

4. **Incorrect** **Correct**
(i) Even Every
(ii) every all
(iii) many every

11. Sentences

1. (i) **Subject** She **Predicate** did not go to Malaysia.
(ii) **Subject** Ramalal **Predicate** brought the food from the market.
(iii) **Subject** Karan **Predicate** didn't eat vegetables last night.
(iv) **Subject** My friend **Predicate** writes short stories.
(v) **Subject** Ramya **Predicate** did not sing well.

2. (i) He didn't give me a glass of milk.
(ii) The contractor didn't finish the work in one day.
(iii) They did not arrive in the morning.
(iv) He didn't look at the pictures on the wall.
(v) Her performance was very bad.

3. (i) Titanic, the unsinkable ship, sank on its maiden voyage.
(ii) He left for London yesterday.
(iii) Arjun is capable of eating 24 bananas.
(iv) She was a good student of her class.
(v) Carbondioxide is the food that plants consume.

4. (i) Does he go to office at 9 o'clock?
(ii) Does she speak English fluently?
(iii) Does he call his mother everyday?
(iv) Have they promised to pay higher wages?
(v) Doesn't Kanishka like to dance?

5. **Incorrect** **Correct**
(ii) in with
(iii) learning learn
(iv) excelling excel
(v) there their
(vi) but and
(vii) insufficient sufficient
(viii) for against

6. (i) Someone (ii) I
(iii) The planets (iv) He
(v) Monday

12. Active-Passive Voice

1. (i) A pair of boots were bought by Mohan from the showroom.
(ii) A finger was pressed on the boots by Mr Gessler.
(iii) The thief was caught by the police from the railway station.
(iv) The shop was visited by me to place an order.
(v) My shoes were mended by the cobbler in 10 minutes.

2. (i) Mr Wonka invented Vita-Wonk.
(ii) He visited many countries.
(iii) Who taught you to paint?
(iv) An Oompa-Loompa volunteer posted the video on Facebook.
(v) Asha gave her four drops of liquid.
(vi) The flood completely destroyed the city.
(vii) Rajesh ate oranges and apples.
(viii) My teacher gave me a chocolate.
(ix) I will complete the project before the deadline.
(x) My mother visits this temple once in a month.

3. (i) Active voice (ii) Passive voice
(iii) Active voice (iv) Passive voice
(v) Active voice (vi) Active voice
(vii) Active voice (viii) Passive voice
(ix) Active voice (x) Active voice

4. **Incorrect** **Correct**
(i) stolen stole
(ii) break broke
(iii) steal stole
(iv) dent dented
(v) crash crashed
(vi) charge charged

5. (i) being made (ii) answered
(iii) teaches (iv) handed
(v) was inaugurated (vi) be played on
(vii) was broken (viii) been collected
(ix) is made (x) is being constructed

13. Direct and Indirect Speech

1. (i) My teacher says that fire is the result of a chemical reaction.
   (ii) My mother advises me not to play with electrical appliances.
   (iii) A journalist said that the fire-fighters had brought the fire under control.
   (iv) Priya said that she had burnt her hand while cooking food in the kitchen.
   (v) Sanjeev asked me if I could help people suffering from burns.
   (vi) The king requested the hermit to let him work in his place.
   (vii) The hermit said (to the king) that he had already been answered.

   or

   The hermit said that he (the king) had already been answered.
   (viii) The bearded man pleaded with me/them to forgive him.
   (ix) The servant said that his master was busy in his work.
   (x) He told me that he didn't trust me.
2. (i) "What a lovely weather outside!", she remarked.
   (ii) My mother said, "You'll break your neck."
   (iii) "No cake for you.", said the waiter.
   (iv) "What a beautiful piece!" he said.
   (v) I murmured, "Oh! I am sorry."
   (vi) The old man said, "Let's sprinkle the ashes."
3. (i) he, that day (ii) requested
   (iii) that (iv) would
   (v) wished (vi) are, here
   (vii) cannot (viii) he, didn't, her

Worksheet 1

1.
Incorrect	Correct
(a) dramatist	dramatists
(b) who	whom
(c) the	an
(d) whom	who
(e) for	of
(f) had	has
(g) for Englishman	of Englishmen

2.
Incorrect	Correct
(a) that	it
(b) closed	close
(c) or	and
(d) in	into
(e) are	is

3.
Incorrect	Correct
(a) you	we
(b) on	in
(c) contact	contacted
(d) themselves	it
(e) myself	I

4.
Incorrect	Correct
(a) an	the
(b) an	a
(c) a	the
(d) an	a

5.
Incorrect	Correct
(a) rushing	rushed
(b) times	time
(c) her	Him
(d) was	had

Worksheet 2

1.
Before	Missing	After
(a) get	any	job
(b) trust	him	consequently
(c) life	became	a
(d) moved	on	seeing
(e) house	and	asked
(f) him	his	unfortunate

2.
Before	Missing	After
(a) which	is	the
(b) in	that	region
(c) it	was	the
(d) Vashishta	who	created
(e) Sirohi	had given	it
(f) who	used	it
(g) It	is	situated
(h) as	a	place

3.
Before	Missing	After
(a) is	as	old
(b) one	of	the
(c) useful	and	fascinating
(d) contains	many	topics
(e) it	is	difficult
(f) which	comes	from

4.
Before	Missing	After
(a) there	are	various
(b) India	and	most
(c) land	in	Delhi
(d) a	at	the
(e) is	with	packed

5.
Before	Missing	After
(a) week	at	9 am
(b) scooter	for	a
(c) shocked	that	he
(d) I	was	mistaken
(e) It	is	a

Reading

Worksheet 1

1. (iv) promise/oath (v) untie
2. (iv) Sarvepalli Radhakrishnan
   (v) Official

Worksheet 2

1. (iv) initially (v) Demon
2. (iv) Lost (v) Crucial

Worksheet 3

1. (iv) nominated (v) cricketer
2. (iv) strange (v) Punishment

Worksheet 4

1. (iv) Highest (v) Dominance
2. (iv) Unaware (v) Imitating

Worksheet 5

1. (i) (c) (ii) (b) (iii) (a) (iv) (c) (v) (d)
2. (i) (b) (ii) (c) (iii) (a) (iv) (d) (v) (a)

Worksheet 6

1. (i) (b) (ii) (b) (iii) (c) (iv) (d) (v) (a)
2. (i) (c) (ii) (b) (iii) (d) (iv) (a) (v) (c)

Worksheet 7

1. (iv) unhappy (v) maid
2. (v) (a) see, fee (b) phase, praise
   (c) bring, ding

Worksheet 8

1. (i) (b) (ii) (c) (iii) (b) (iv) (d) (v) (b)
2. (i) (b) (ii) (c) (iii) (a) (iv) (d) (v) (c)